COLLINGWOOD

Northumberland's Heart of Oak

Max Adams

Tyne Bridge Publishing

Acknowledgments

The author would like to thank the following:
The Winston Churchill Memorial Trust for generously supporting my travels and research. Mrs Susan Collingwood Cameron, for allowing me access to her papers and for her enthusiasm and hospitality. Senor Fransco Pons Mantorani of the Hotel del Almirante in Menorca, for many kindnesses. The many people who helped me in various ways in my travels: the Sarullo family of Palermo; Mike and Lindsay Kiesseling and Mrs Hyacinth Hale of English Harbour; Bill and Wendy Westman of Boston and Sally Gardner of Wellfleet; Stephen and Christina Stead of Purley. Mary Wimpress and Ian Lennox supported the project at all stages. I would also like to thank Mr Clive Richards and Trinity House, Newcastle for permission to use photographs in their collections, and finally Anna Flowers of Tyne Bridge Publishing.

Tyne Bridge Publishing would also like to thank Denis Gowans and Dick Keys for their helpful advice and historical information; and Ian Whitehead of Tyne & Wear Museums.

Illustrations are reproduced from the collections of Newcastle Libraries unless otherwise indicated.

© **Max Adams**, 2005, 2009
ISBN: 978 1 85795 132 5

Published by
City of Newcastle upon Tyne
Newcastle Libraries
Tyne Bridge Publishing
2005, revised 2009

www.tynebridgepublishing.co.uk

Printed by Elanders Hindson, North Tyneside

A more extensive life of Lord Collingwood can be read in *Admiral Collingwood: Nelson's Own Hero* by Max Adams, published by Weidenfeld & Nicolson, 2005.

Contents

WHEN ENGLAND SETS her banner forth
And bids her armour shine,
She'll not forget the famous North,
The lads of moor and Tyne;
And when the loving cup's in hand,
And honour leads the cry,
They know not old Northumberland
Who'll pass her memory by.

When Nelson sailed for Trafalgar
With all his country's best,
He held them dear as brothers are,
But one beyond the rest.
For when the fleet with heroes manned
To clear the decks began,
The boast of old Northumberland
He sent to lead the van.

Himself by Victory's bulwarks stood
And cheered to see the sight;
'That noble fellow Collingwood,
How bold he goes to fight!'
Love, that the league of Ocean spanned,
Heard him as face to face;
'What would he give, Northumberland,
To share our pride of place?'

The flag that goes the world around
And flaps on every breeze
Has never gladdened fairer ground
Or kinder hearts than these.
So when the loving cup's in hand
And honour leads the cry,
They know not old Northumberland,
Who'll pass her memory by.

Northumberland
By Sir Henry Newbolt

Foreword

CUTHBERT COLLINGWOOD, if he were alive today, might be a stern but kindly headmaster: old-fashioned in some respects, forward-looking in others; rarely adored but always admired, and with affection. If he was a hero, it was in spite of himself, and because of the state of the world into which he was born. That he was a remarkable man was recognised by all those who knew him well, and by a few others whose lives he affected. His closest friend Horatio Nelson, ten years his junior, saw in him all the virtues that made up the exemplary Englishman: selfless devotion to duty, integrity, love of one's family, sense of justice, humanity, humour, and utterly fearless physical bravery. Collingwood was, in a sense, Nelson's ideal – just as Nelson himself was Collingwood's.

Collingwood was far from perfect. He was grumpy and short-tempered, suffered fools not at all, was economical to the point of parsimony, and more than slightly pompous. He was a hopeless delegator – what we would nowadays call a control freak: his attention to detail was legendary. There is also an element of tragedy in his story, especially in his last years. And he disliked change, especially political change.

But, for all his conservatism there is something remarkably modern about him. His decisions were always based on what he thought was right, and devil take those who cared how it looked; his leadership skills would have modern management gurus nodding their heads with approval. His throw-away jokes are the stuff of stand-up comedy.

I find it impossible not to like him. I hope that Northumbrians, who do not know him as well as they should, will come to like him too.

Max Adams, 2005

The sights and sounds of ships on the Tyne must have been central to young Cuthbert Collingwood's experience as he grew up just yards from the riverside, between St Nicholas' Cathedral and the Black Gate. This view was drawn by Nathanial Buck in 1745.

Newcastle 1748-1760

For much of the 18th century Britain was at war. So Cuthbert Collingwood – first son of a Newcastle trader – grew up in a warlike world. He was born in a house on The Side within a few yards of city walls which had been manned against the Scots as recently as 1745, and under the shadow of the New Castle built by William the Conqueror's oldest son Robert. Barely noticed these days, The Side then was a busy, steep little street nestling below the medieval cathedral and Black Gate, its tall houses jutting out so far that it can have had little sun.

In 1756, when Collingwood was eight years old, Britain declared war against France. Newspapers of the time were full of the war. There were constant threats of invasion, rumours of plots and intrigue. There was also gossip from across the Seven Seas to be heard anywhere along the Quayside where ships of war, merchantmen and colliers were constantly coming and going. And just as children today play out their fantasies in computer games, boys of that era would have replayed famous naval engagements with their friends – as indeed sailors themselves did – using crumbs of bread and biscuit to represent ships on the kitchen tablecloth.

The sea was a huge element in the life of 18th-century Newcastle, but it was not the only element. Newcastle was above all a coal town, whose prosperity was beginning to reap civic benefits. A turnpike road to Morpeth had just been built by the Corporation; new thoroughfares like Pilgrim

'The future admiral', an 18th century print.

Street were being laid out, and springs tapped to supply mains water to the town; Newcastle had its own bank; wagon ways laced their way across the countryside down to the Tyne to be met by keels, and across the region there was a buzz of engineering, industrial and agricultural innovation: steam engines were being used to pump water from mines and cattle of prodigious size were being bred on Northumberland's lush pastures. The first gaslights were about to be demonstrated in Newcastle. John Wesley came here to preach to large crowds, and liked the place: 'If I did not believe there was another world I should spend all my summers here' he wrote; and Daniel Defoe had long since described, for a London audience, the sight of 'Mountains of Coals', wondering at the same time where all the people lived who consumed them.

The news was full of strikes and riots too. Keelmen struck many times for an increase in their wages. In Sunderland a group of men who had been caught by the press gang escaped and caused mayhem, and on another occasion the press gang themselves were committed to Newgate prison for assault and other riotous behaviour at 'Ewesburn'. Amidst worrying news from France and the colonies, silly season rules operated in the press then, as now:

Two dyers, who were washing cloth at the river, were thrown into the water and both drowned, by a sheep which leaped from the quay into the water, being pursued by a dog down one of the narrow entries in the close…

This was Cuthbert Collingwood's world at the start of his eleventh year: 1759. In the very few books which have been written about him, it is always said that he and John

The Side photographed around 1860. Collingwood's birthplace was just on the corner towards the top of the slope, on the right, on a site now occupied by Milburn House. The narrow lane was once the main thoroughfare up through the town from the Quayside.

Scott (later Lord Eldon, the Lord Chancellor) were pupils at the Royal Grammar School – then a free school for children of respectable but poor families, supported by the town's Corporation. It is true, but it would be wrong to call Collingwood a product of that institution because he was there for less than a year. He was taught Latin and Greek, and knew his bible; but his later learning was acquired in the cabins of men of war.

Collingwood's family was an old one, steeped in the Northumbrian countryside, but his particular branch was neither landed nor wealthy. An earlier Sir Cuthbert had been a famous Border reiver, though more unlucky than successful, having been kidnapped by the Scots. The Admiral's father, also Cuthbert, had been apprenticed to a trader and then gone into business for himself, but was not very successful. There was no naval history in the family, but they, like many people in a country where five percent of the male popula-tion were seafarers of one sort or another, knew naval peo-ple, even if they were not particularly well-connected. A young boy thinking of the sea might have gone into the mer-chant navy, where wages were high and he might make a fine living in one of Britain's colonies. But this 11-year-old had other ideas.

The year 1759 was The Year of Victories. Though the British Army won a stunning victory over the French at Minden, it was the Navy, forever expanding and protecting the trading interests of the empire, that seemed constantly in action. In the late 18th century, news was dislocated from events by a variety of capricious fates: tides, weather, acci-dents and the speed at which ships could sail. Economic and military advantage was gained from the early arrival of news, and land-based telegraph systems would play a key role in

The house where Collingwood was born in 1748 photographed in the late 19th century.

intelligence during the Napoleonic Wars. But until the arrival of the steam vessel, nothing could overcome a contrary wind or tide.

In June of that year Admiral Hawke sailed with a fleet to the Mediterranean to join Admiral Boscawen in a blockade of French ports, and there was a report on General Wolfe's expedition to force a passage up the St. Lawrence River in Canada. A list of the French and English fleets at Toulon was published, and Collingwood, his younger brothers Wilfred and John, and their sisters too, would have learned their names, their Captains, the number of their guns and their rigs by heart. Convincing nautical phrases like 'the weather-gage', 'hull-down' and '32-pounder' would certainly have tripped off their tongues. But although the French fleet came out of Toulon, it sailed back in again without being brought to battle.

In August the French fleet in Brest thought the British were coming in to get them, though the roar of gunfire that they heard was only Hawke's celebration of the news of victory at Minden. But in the September 15th edition of the weekly *Courant*, a *Gazette Extraordinary* received by the Admiralty in London was published in full, bringing news the country had been waiting for: Boscawen's fleet had caught up with the French between Cape St Vincent and Lagos, off the south-west corner of Spain, and defeated them in a major battle, taking three ships of the line and burning two others.

Then in October came news of the dramatic capture of Quebec and heroic death of General Wolfe on the Heights of Abraham. And in November Admiral Hawke came up with the French fleet off Quiberon Bay and chased them through dangerous shoals in a gale of shocking force, bringing them

to action and defeating them decisively: three French ships were wrecked, two foundered, and one was captured; her value, in accordance with tradition, divided amongst the crews of the victorious British ships as prize money. Small wonder, perhaps, that the 11-year-old Cuthbert Collingwood was drawn to the sea and its potential for heroics and glory.

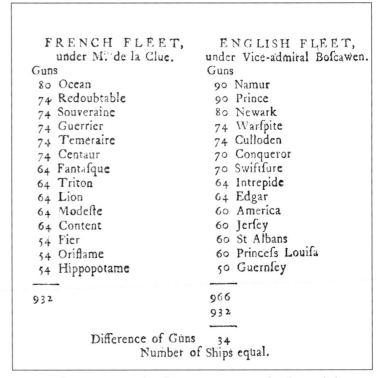

FRENCH FLEET, under M. de la Clue.	ENGLISH FLEET, under Vice-admiral Boscawen.
Guns	Guns
80 Ocean	90 Namur
74 Redoubtable	90 Prince
74 Souveraine	80 Newark
74 Guerrier	74 Warspite
74 Temeraire	74 Culloden
74 Centaur	70 Conqueror
64 Fantasque	70 Swiftsure
64 Triton	64 Intrepide
64 Lion	64 Edgar
64 Modeste	60 America
64 Content	60 Jersey
54 Fier	60 St Albans
54 Oriflame	60 Princess Louisa
54 Hippopotame	50 Guernsey
932	966
	932
Difference of Guns 34	
Number of Ships equal.	

Newcastle Courant, 28th July 1759, compares the ships of the English and French fleets.

The ropes 1761-1773

In 1761, at the age of twelve, Collingwood entered the navy as a volunteer aboard a 28-gun frigate, the *Shannon*, whose commander, Captain Braithwaite, was an uncle by marriage. Cuthbert Snr. paid £30 for him to be introduced to a society which by today's standards seems unbelievably harsh, brutal, dangerous and unpleasant. For Collingwood, of the 49 years left until his death, 44 would be spent at sea. He would have to get used to it.

A 28-gun frigate of His Majesty's Navy was a ship of about 500 tons, with a deck-length of 110 feet or so not including the bowsprit, and a beam of just over 30 feet. The guns would have been 9-pounders, 14 to a side, giving her a broadside weight – the mass of cannon balls she could discharge in one broadside – of 126lb. She would carry a crew of over 200 men with 18 officers, including two lieutenants, a sailing master, gunner, bosun, carpenters, surgeon, and four midshipmen. Collingwood was one of these last – the lowest form of life aboard a ship and frequently reminded of it, even though he had the right to report for punishment seamen of vast experience three times his age.

Very quickly, Collingwood had to learn the ropes: 30 miles of them. Futtock shrouds, tacks, bowlines, sheets, cross-catharpins, backstays, forestays, shrouds, ratlines and many more, often with archaic and sometimes silly-sounding names like 'timenoguy'. There were masts and sails to comprehend: mizzen, main and fore: topmasts, topgallant masts; courses, spritsails, skyscrapers, bonnets, studdingsails and staysails. In almost any manoeuvre at sea complicated combinations of all these things had to be controlled with perfection.

The midshipmen's berth was cramped, dark, revoltingly smelly and fetid, running with a combination of water, general filth and rats (on long voyages midshipmen would hunt them down and eat them as food supplies ran low). Midshipmen were the future officers of the Royal Navy and, in addition to their duties in charge of the seamen, were expected to learn to steer and sail a ship, take navigational readings, survey ports and harbours and handle guns, so that eventually they might pass for lieutenant. Collingwood later became as famous for his educating and handling of midshipmen as he was for his many other qualities.

In optimal conditions frigates – lightly armed and built for speed – could make something over 10 or 12 knots (about 11-14mph). They were comparatively manoeuvrable, but even so they could not point closer to the wind than 67 degrees (imagine a clock: you want to go towards the twelve, but cannot aim closer than two or 10 o'clock) which meant that sailing upwind involved endless tacking: zig-zagging in a slow and cumbersome slalom motion.

A man of war had to carry enough men to sail the ship under any set of possible conditions, and to fight her at the same time. Each gun required a crew of six to eight men to fire, clean and reload it and with a gun – even a small frigate's 9-pounder – weighing a ton and a half, and with an awesome recoil, the men had to be either very experienced, or learn fast. In a heavy sea guns, when out of control, could smash through a ship's side; and injuries were frequent, caused by crushing, exploding barrels, and enemy fire. Splinters were perhaps the worst, much like shrapnel from a bomb. The job of a midshipman like Collingwood, in action, would be to look after the crews of several guns, ensuring they had enough powder and shot, and redistribute them when men were injured or killed, or when guns were put out of action.

The diet of a seaman in the Georgian navy was notorious: biscuit as hard as rock and full of weevils (bitter to the taste) or grubs (cold on the tongue); salt meat that was often so old and hard that spare parts for the ship could be fashioned from it; water that was rank after a few weeks at sea, and cheese that was so putrid only rats would touch it. All these things are true, but they are not the whole story. For one thing, the sailors' diet has to be compared with that available to landsmen. It may have been less fresh, but in

The Sailor's Farewell, by C. Mosley, 1743, gives a romantic glimpse of the midshipman's world below decks. Note the square gun port.

quantity it was generous: six pounds of meat per week, for example, to each man. When in foreign waters the diet would often be supplemented with fresh fish and local fruit and vegetables, and although the beer and rum issue was enough to ensure a state of semi-permanent drunkenness, it was laced with lime to help prevent scurvy, and almost all captains of Collingwood's day realised the importance of diet in maintaining the health of their crews.

Whether a young midshipman like Collingwood thrived or not depended on many things: his character, his messmates, the captain and officers under whom he served and perhaps, above all, on luck. Many couldn't take it, many more were simply unfit for its hardships. Collingwood was lucky in one sense. Braithwaite, his commander, was capable and decent, and ensured that he learnt the ways of the ship without undue humiliation, lessons that he himself would pass on.

A midshipman could not be considered for his first, crucial promotion to lieutenant until he had been at least six years at sea; then he had to pass a severe examination at the Admiralty. And very often, in that age, he had to 'pass for a gentleman' too. Commanders like James Cook, another North-Easterner, were a rarity in having, as Collingwood himself approvingly put it, 'come through the port hole rather than the cabin window'.

We know little about Collingwood's career in these early years. What we do know is that he was conscientious and proved himself a highly capable seaman. Between 1761 and 1773 he served in at least five ships: *Shannon*; the frigates *Gibraltar* and *Liverpool* in which he kept a log that survives; *Lennox*, a much larger ship, of 70 guns; and *Portland*, a fourth-rate two-decker of 50 guns, from whose voyage we have another log.

Left: a midshipman, and right a lieutenant, late 18th century.

Shannon was mainly employed in Home and Atlantic waters, though once the war ended there was little chance of any action in her. In *Gibraltar*, also commanded by Braithwaite, Collingwood made his first trip to the Mediterranean. His younger brother Wilfred served alongside him in all three ships. In *Liverpool* he made the first of many visits to Port Mahon, on the south-east coast of Menorca. The British possessed Menorca for much of the 18th century. It was and is one of the finest natural harbours in the Mediterranean, long and sheltered and very deep (100ft or so) right up to the quayside. On this commission, having been promoted to the rank of master's mate, he completed a survey of the harbour.

In *Portland* in 1773 Collingwood made his first journey to the West Indies. This station was notorious in the service, mainly because of the climate – malaria and yellow fever were rife – but partly because of that and the high incidence of piracy, a young sailor had a better chance of promotion here than on many another station. No such luck for Collingwood, though. Intriguingly, he later recalled that this was the year he met Nelson and in which they began an extraordinary friendship that would last 32 years.

While Collingwood languished in dull and dangerous service, the world was moving on. At Newcastle, that winter of 1773, the River Tyne froze four miles below the bridge (a temporary wooden structure; the famous medieval bridge, with all its houses, had been swept away by a terrible flood two years earlier) and a skating match took place on it. Mozart, aged eight had already performed before the young King George III; HMS *Victory* had been launched and James Watt had patented his steam engine.

There was peace, of sorts, in Europe. But in 1773 rumblings of discontent in the colonies across the Atlantic were already making ripples at home. This was the year of the Boston Tea Party, when a dispute about unfair import duties culminated in a group of young men dressed up as native Indians tossing a load of British tea into Boston harbour. By the end of the year the British army garrison and loyalist inhabitants of the city were virtually under siege, and dependent on the navy to supply them. As a result, Collingwood finally got his chance for a slice of glory not at sea, but in a land battle: he was to be a first-hand witness of, and participant in, the American War of Independence.

Weapons of mass destruction: ships, guns, and crews of the Georgian navy

Ships by rate

Rate: the 'rate' denoted the six orders into which ships of war were divided into, according to their size and strength.

First rate: all ships of 100 guns and more, having 42-pounders on the lower deck, down to 6-pounders on the quarterdeck and forecastle. They were manned with over 850 men including officers, seamen, marines, servants and others.

Second rate: ships carrying from 90-98 guns.

Third rate: ships carrying from 64-84 guns.

Fourth rate: ships carrying 44-60 guns; by Collingwood's day these were considered too light to sail in the line of battle.

Fifth rate: frigates mounting from 32-40 or even 60 guns.

Sixth rate: anything smaller with a captain (usually 24-28 guns). Those under a commander were called sloops.

Guns and crews

Broadsides could deliver over 1000 pounds of shot. Guns were rated by weight of shot, usually 32-pounders on the lower deck, 24- and 18-pounders on the mid and upper deck. The upper deck might also have carronades (lighter cannon) firing shot up to 68 pounds over a short range.

A captain, c.1797.

Shot could be two balls linked by a short chain to bring down rigging, a container of musket balls, or even heated shot to start fires.

Gun crews practised until they could run in the gun, load the cartridge, a wad of cloth, the iron shot, another wad all down the muzzle, run the gun out, fire, worm and sponge (to remove any trace of burning cartridge) reload and run out, all, ideally, within 90 seconds on a heavy rolling deck.

Captains tried to 'cross the T' – range up across the enemy's stern and fire so that shot would sweep the length of the gun decks, splinters would fly, gun tackles would part and guns roll loose.

Boston 1774-1775

There were enlightened men, as well as interested money-makers on both sides of the Atlantic, who deplored the breach between Britain and the New World. But George III was implacable. In May 1774 the *Boston & Country Gazette* (a 'rebel' newspaper) reported news from London that a Boston Port Bill was to be passed blockading all trade from that city:

Concerning public matters, I am sorry to say that Things are going from bad to worse, and a breach between Great Britain & her colonies seems approaching very fast. This accursed tea is the very match that is appointed to set fire to a Train of Gun Powder.

And so it proved. By the end of 1773 British and loyalist Bostonians were virtually besieged in the city's peninsula. Before massive later land clearance it was connected to the mainland by a narrow spit of low lying land. The stand-off only entrenched more deeply the stubborn attitudes of both sides. The train of gunpowder, once lit, would lead to independence for the colonies from Great Britain after a bitter eight-year war.

Collingwood was 26 when he sailed in *Preston*, a 50-gun ship, with Admiral Graves. They arrived in Boston on 2 July 1774. Their role was to support the beleaguered Army generals. Collingwood, without influence or wealth, was already

old for a master's mate (a senior rank for a midshipman, but crucially short of an officer's commission). By now he had been longer at sea than on land, and was evidently a fine sailor, navigator and surveyor. But he had never seen anything like proper action and must have thought that he would end his naval career without ever being promoted. All that would change in 1775. In April came Lexington and Concord, humiliating defeats for the British against small guerrilla forces in the countryside of Massachusetts.

The battle at Bunker's Hill (it was actually fought on Breed's Hill) took place because British Army generals decided to break out of Boston and show the colonials who was in charge. But the secret got out – Boston was full of rebel spies – and well before the British were ready to move the Massachusetts militia, ill-equipped and led as they were, had fortified a small redoubt on Breed's

Hill on the Charlestown Peninsula, within sight (and shot) of British batteries in Boston, and of her navy's ships in the Inner Harbour and Charles River.

All through the night of June 16th 1775 the rebels dug (a British officer heard strange noises and reported them, but nothing was done). At first light the following morning HMS *Lively* opened fire on the entrenchments, but could not elevate her guns high enough to do more than blow the head off a single rebel. The senior British commander, General Howe, then ordered his Redcoats to re-take the Charlestown Peninsula – just as one might order tea and scones. Two waves of Redcoats were mown down by rebels who, short of ammunition, water, food and reinforcements, were ordered by their commander, Colonel William Prescott, not to shoot until they saw the whites of the British eyes. The Redcoats suffered more than a thousand casualties, though their third wave just managed to retake the rebel positions.

It was master's mate Cuthbert Collingwood who was sent by Admiral Graves to command the boats that took the reinforcements across to Charlestown, then re-supply them and take off the wounded as they arrived back at the beach – under fire not just from rebel positions on the hill, but at risk from shore batteries in Boston. His coolness, good judgement and bravery won him his promotion, though for the British Army, technically victorious, it was a day of abject humiliation.

Although the British regained the Charlestown Peninsula, their commanders were in such a state of shock that they failed to consolidate their gains, retreating again to Boston, which became their last continental redoubt. Nine months later they evacuated the city, and within a year America declared independence at Philadelphia.

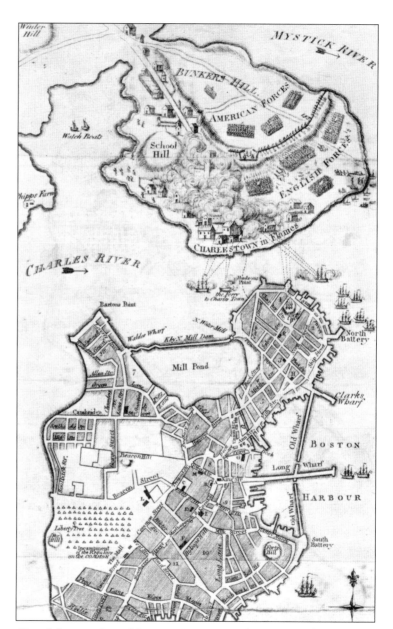

Detail from a plan of Boston, 1775, printed in Newcastle in 1778. Across the Charles River. is Charlestown, and Bunker's Hill.

War by other means 1777-1786

For much of the year 1776 Lieutenant Cuthbert Collingwood was in London. Although he was desperate to go north to be with his family (his father had died while he was in Boston), if he left London, with so many other young officers also trying to get employment, he would lose all chance of another ship. So there he stayed, while news from the colonies worsened almost by the month. Although the British took New York in September, they were defeated by Washington at Trenton, New Jersey in December.

Newcastle was as concerned with the war as the rest of the country. Its burgesses, dismayed by the American situation as Collingwood was (the loss of trade was potentially disastrous) petitioned the King to bring an end to the conflict. His Majesty was unmoved. There had been another hard winter in the North-East too, with the Tyne frozen completely as far up as Newburn. But development continued, with the construction of the Assembly Rooms close to Collingwood's old school on Westgate Road, and the building of the City Road to the East allowing traffic to reach Heaton and North Shields without the climb up Pandon Bank.

Collingwood at last got a ship, but must have been disappointed that it wasn't a more glamorous posting. *Hornet* was a 14-gun sloop, the smallest type of ship in the navy. She was sent to the West Indies to join the Jamaica station where, if he survived rampant disease, Collingwood might expect fur-

ther promotion. But his hopes were dashed, for *Hornet* had a rotten captain. Her commander was Lieutenant Robert Haswell, a mean and vindictive man embittered by his failure to make 'post'. Just as midshipmen dreamed of becoming lieutenants, so lieutenants dreamed of making the step up to post captain. For once there, they established a position on the conveyor belt that would one day make them an admiral, if they survived long enough. Haswell had been a lieutenant for 18 years without making post, and although that might simply have been a matter of bad luck, in Collingwood's view he was a poor officer whose conduct bordered on cowardice:

What a country is this at present to make a fortune in; all kinds of people wallowing in their wealth acquired by prizes and so extraordinary an exception are we that to be as unfortunate as the Hornet is become a proverbial saying, and the Black girls sing our poverty in their ludicrous songs…

For the first time, a picture of the adult Collingwood can be drawn. Like most other officers in the navy he was zealous, desperate for glory and fortune, and if he loathed anything more than the enemy it was a bad senior officer, incapable of commanding respect. Collingwood later admitted to a fiery temper, and despite his vulnerable position as a lieutenant, he provoked Haswell into court-martialling him. Two years after Bunker's Hill, he might have found himself dismissed from the navy forever for disobedience and neglect of orders. So he must have got a grim sense of satisfaction from the fact that, although acquitted, he was admonished 'for want of cheerfulness and alacrity'.

In 1778 Horatio Nelson arrived in the West Indies in *Lowestoffe*, a 32-gun frigate commanded by William Locker, a captain as unlike Haswell as it was possible to conceive: brave, considerate, active, and admired by both officers and men. Nelson, still only 19 (ten years younger than Collingwood), but with political influence at home and talents that were already obvious, was promoted to lieutenant on Sir Peter Parker's flagship, and Collingwood was released from his torment by replacing Nelson in *Lowestoffe*. Nelson's mercurial rise continued as he was made 'master and commander' in *Badger*, a 14-gun brig, and then given his irreversible step up to post captain in *Hinchinbroke*, a 28-gun frigate. His magnetism already apparent, he seemed to tow his friend Collingwood in his wake, as the former master's mate, now 30, was

A page from Collingwood's log for Sunday 2nd May 1778 showing the approach to Port Royal, Jamaica.

made commander in *Badger*, and then post captain in *Hinchinbroke*. Sir Peter Parker, as both the new captains acknowledged, was a great promoter of talent, and under him they flourished, gaining the confidence needed to take on the responsibility of command in His Majesty's Navy.

Britain was technically at war with both France and Spain over their support for the Americans, and it was now for the first time that Nelson got himself – and Collingwood – involved in one of those amphibious scrapes that would blight his whole career. An expedition was sent up the San Juan River in what is now Nicaragua to see if a route could be forced through to the Pacific Ocean (where James Cook, on his third voyage of discovery, had recently been murdered by Hawaiian islanders). It was badly planned, and went disastrously wrong as a Spanish garrison put up unexpected resistance, and the dangers of the jungle saw men dropping in their dozens. Nelson, ordered to provide naval support, instead became the expedition's effective military leader, and very nearly died of exhaustion and fever before he was evacuated and sent back to England. Collingwood, stationed in support at the mouth of the river, was lucky: he was one of only 20 left alive on his ship after 180 men and officers died from malaria and yellow fever, the infamous Yellow Jack.

The expedition was a step backwards for both captains, and for Collingwood worse was to come. A year later, in 1781, he was given the 24-gun frigate *Pelican*, but she was wrecked in a hurricane off the Morant Keys in Jamaica. He got his men ashore by making rafts out of the wreckage, and ten days later they were taken off by another frigate. Such exploits are the stuff of legend, but typically, Collingwood made nothing of his own heroics. Now without a ship, he returned to England and again stayed in London where his

Horatio Nelson

chances of getting another command were better than they would be 300 miles to the north.

In the summer of 1783 Collingwood was given command of *Mediator*, a 44-gun fourth-rate ship of the line, in effect a heavy frigate, but had trouble finding enough men for her – a constant problem for the navy. *Mediator* was bound for the West Indies, and she carried as passengers the new Navy Commissioner for the Leeward Islands, based in Antigua: John Moutray and his much younger wife Mary.

Antigua was strategically important as the north-eastern-most island in the Caribbean. It was a rich possession for the

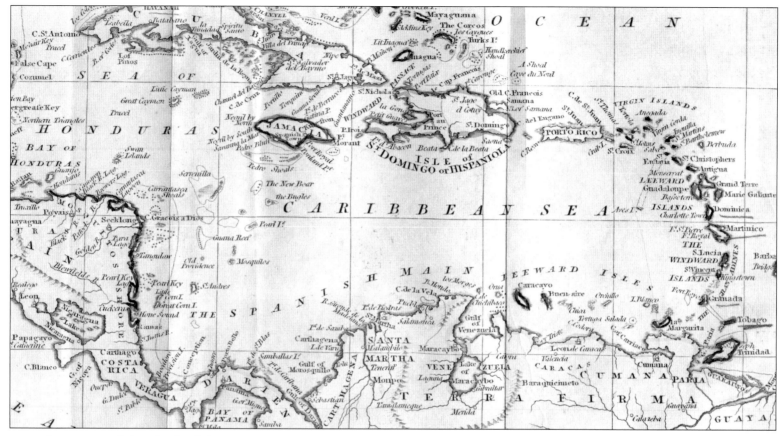

Central America and the islands of the Caribbean from Hewson Clarke's History of the War, 1816. The San Juan river, in what is now Nicaragua, is just north of the name Costa Rica.

British – its wealth coming from sugar grown on highly developed estates, totally dependent on slavery. Compared with Menorca, another vital island possession, the island was easy to defend. Reefs confined shipping (and any hostile landing parties) to St Johns in the north-west, and English Harbour and Falmouth in the south. Of these, English Harbour was the most important. It had first been used by the navy in the 17th century. It had a narrow entrance, easily defended with small forts on either side, and the inner harbour could not be seen from the sea. Although not deep like Port Mahon, it made a perfect careening station and was virtually hurricane-proof as an anchorage. By 1725 land at what is now called Nelson's Dockyard (the only working Georgian dockyard left in the world) had been bought by the navy to establish a dockyard there.

In 1784 Nelson came out to join Collingwood in *Boreas*, a 28-gun frigate. Together with Collingwood's brother Wilfred, in the sloop *Rattler*, they set about enforcing the Navigation Acts in the islands, an activity that won them no friends and a number of formidable enemies. The Acts, dating back to the days of Oliver Cromwell, stated that British colonies could only trade with the mother country or other colonies. Since America was no longer a colony, the islands that continued to trade with her did so illegally. That was the view of Nelson and the two Collingwoods. The governors and merchants of the West Indies, who profited from this trade, naturally enough disagreed.

English Harbour, Antigua, the Georgian dockyard from Shirley Heights.

Quite who it was that initiated the crack-down on this smuggling is a matter of dispute between historians. After the end of the hurricane season of 1784 Collingwood (by his own statement) or Nelson (by his) prevented an American vessel from entering St Johns. Under a well-known ruse, merchant captains would request permission to dock for repairs.

Collingwood offered the services of his carpenter to effect the alleged repairs, and impounded the cargo, while the American master went ashore to complain to the governor, Thomas Shirley – who, like Admiral Hughes, the station's senior officer, seems to have more or less connived in the illicit trade.

Once again Collingwood and Nelson were in their element, defending their country's interests with zeal, and in the face of an injustice. While there was little chance of glory or serious action, they knew they were doing their duty, and their friendship became firmer than ever. They drew each other's portraits, and developed a mutual admiration. They also developed a strong admiration for Mary Moutray. She and her husband lived in a house on Windsor Hill overlooking the dockyard (all that is left of the house now are a few stone foundations and scatters of broken china, bottles, and whelk shells). Whenever Nelson and Collingwood were at English Harbour – either during the hurricane months or when their ships' hulls were being scraped clean at the careening station – they were invited to dine with the Moutrays. John Moutray was elderly and sick, as Collingwood told his sister:

Clive Richards

Detail from a portrait of Mary Moutray.

Commissioner Moutray has but ill health. I am afraid we shall lose them; they are very desirous to get home, and if he is not recall'd I think he will resign. I shall miss them grievously, she is quite a delight and makes many an hour cheerful, that without her wou'd be dead weight.

Nelson had even warmer things to say about his 'dear sweet friend', who was 'very, very good to me' and evidently the relationship of the three became intimate – they would frizz her hair for her before a ball, and she would tease them – though there is no suggestion of any impropriety. But they both remained close friends with her in later years: Collingwood – tall and handsome and healthy, compared with Nelson who was slight and carried a permanent sickly hue from his many fevers – was still writing to her what can only be described as romantic letters. For her part, Mary Moutray was able to coax Collingwood out of the reserve so natural to a man used to his own company in the loneliness of a great ship's cabin. She wrote:

There was a degree of reserve in his manner which prevented the playfulness of his imagination and his powers of adding charm to private society being duly appreciated. But the intimacy of a long voyage gave us the good fortune to know him as he was, so that, after our arrival in Antigua, he was as a beloved brother in our house.

Collingwood, returning to England in 1786, was now to spend the longest period of his life at home in Northumberland, without a ship or even the remote prospect of one, but happy in the bosom of his family, and able to walk again through the hills, woods and pastures of his beloved Northumberland.

Pockets full of acorns 1787-1793

On the 20th April laſt, in the Weſt Indies, Captain Wilfred Collingwood, Commander of his Majeſty's Ship Rattler. By his death his friends have loſt a moſt valuable and affectionate relative, and his country an active and zealous Officer.

Collingwood's brother Wilfred was dead. In May 1787 Cuthbert received a very touching, typically affectionate letter from Nelson, with the news that Wilfred, worn out and perhaps carrying some disease, had died while on his way from English Harbour to Grenada in April. Collingwood's reaction to this awful news is not known. From 1786 to 1790 just one of his letters survives. He was now at home with his family, and his correspondence dried up – though there must have been letters to the Admiralty asking vainly for a ship. Collingwood made the best of these years on half-pay. He got to know relations he had barely seen since he was a midshipman: his brother John, his sisters, and the large network of Collingwoods and collateral relations that were scattered across the North-East, from Chirton and Gateshead in the south to Morpeth, and Musselburgh near Edinburgh.

While he had been away Newcastle, and indeed the whole country, was experiencing social and industrial change on a grand scale. There was now a Royal Mail coach running between London and Newcastle. Dean Street was in the process of being made by the removal of the old arch of the Low Bridge. The first mechanical threshers, just invented by the brilliant Scottish millwright Andrew Meikle, were about to whirr into action on farms across the region, altering forever a pattern of secure but soul-destroying rural labour.

Fortunately, the lack of alternative employment in the south that would lead to rick burning and riots was contrasted in the North-East by increased employment to be found in mining, shipping and other industrial and agricultural developments. Newcastle's heyday would not come for another 20 years (George Stephenson was born in 1781; John Buddle in 1773; William Hedley in 1779), but Northumberland's farmers had been innovating for a generation, and Fat Cattle and Teeswater sheep were already being bred to the amazement of the world. Elsewhere brilliant industrialists and innovators like Wedgewood, Priestley, Boulton and Watt, were introducing new ideas in production, transport and society: everywhere the march of progress, for good or ill. On one hand were the beginnings of mass unemployment, riots, and peasants turned off their land by Enclosure Acts; on the other, the stirrings of liberalism – Tom Paine, Adam Smith, and the Society for the Suppression of the Slave Trade. Collingwood was fascinated by all of this, and his later career shows him to have been innovative and progressive in managing men, but his basic political instincts were cast-iron Tory.

The deeply dependable uncertainties of the sea must have made Collingwood and all the other half-pay captains look

The improved Teeswater sheep engraved by Collingwood's contemporary, Thomas Bewick.

wistfully to the continent for another war. They would have to wait for five years. But if Collingwood could do little to advance his own career, England's future was never far from his mind. He famously, when walking among the hills and fields of Northumberland, filled his pockets with acorns to plant in hedgerows and patches of waste land, so that the navy would never again want for oak trees to build her ships with.

She would need them. Social upheaval in France, long seen in England as a domestic matter, now exploded in a revolution that England could not ignore for very long. There was hostility too from across the Atlantic: John Paul Jones, expatriate American naval hero-cum-pirate, was harrying the North-East coast, on one occasion firing a cannon ball at the church in Alnmouth (it missed, bounced three times across a

field and landed finally on the roof of a farmhouse). At the same time it looked as though there would be war with Spain over trading and whaling rights off the north-west coast of America.

Collingwood went to London and took rooms in Dean Street, at the heart of Soho, from where he made applications to the Admiralty for a ship, using all the influence that his experience and reputation could muster. He must already have made an impression because he was indeed offered a ship, while Nelson, back home in Norfolk with his new wife, was not. In 1790 Collingwood was given *Mermaid*, a 28-gun frigate. He spent the winter of 1790-91 in the West Indies on a cruise (a pleasant commission which gave an enterprising captain a very free rein), while the war of the so-called Spanish Armament fizzled to nothing. It was the last carefree period in a life which, very soon, would be dedicated to one single ambition: defeat of the French. It also gave Collingwood a chance to get to know his new companion, Bounce:

My dog is a charming creature, every body admires him but he is grown as tall as the table I am writing on almost.

We do not know what sort of dog Bounce was, though he nearly had his 'picture taken' many years later in Cadiz, but over the years Collingwood's letters to his family, and glowing endorsements from Collingwood's men, give us an idea of what he was like. Large and strong, certainly, for Bounce was famous for swimming behind Collingwood's boat when his master was being rowed ashore. He slept next to Collingwood's cot and, captain or admiral, Collingwood would sing him to sleep with songs that he composed himself. Bounce was the perfect naval dog – Collingwood thought him more intelligent and enterprising than some of his officers – except for one thing. He hated the sound of gunfire. This was a distinct disadvantage in a dog whose master was dedicated to achieving perfection in the art of naval gunnery. Bounce learned to hide among the decks below the waterline whenever he heard the sound of the marine's drum beating to quarters.

It was obviously the time in Collingwood's life for making long-term commitments (he was now 42), for he also married. His bride was Sarah Blackett, daughter of the Mayor of Newcastle and well-connected with other Northumberland families such as the Roddams. They were married in 1791 at St Nicholas' Cathedral in Newcastle, and went to live in a rented house on Oldgate in Morpeth, close by the banks of the River Wansbeck. This house they later bought, and it remains to be seen today, a sober but respectable squarish townhouse of red brick. Within two years they had daughters – Sarah (little Sal) and Mary Patience, on whom Collingwood doted. In a short time his duty would take him to sea again, and he would miss most of their childhood, but they remained his greatest solace in the troubles to come.

Britain's chief initial interest in the French Revolution was a concern that it would spread to England. Such fears were reinforced by trouble at home: The seamen of Shields – over 1000 of them – had seized their owners' ships in an attempt to have their wages raised, and a couple of sloops had been sent to deal with them: 'their enthusiasm for liberty' as

Bounce may have been a Spanish Pointer like this one, engraved by Thomas Bewick. Local tradition in Mahon has it that he was a Menorcan rabbit dog.

Collingwood put it, 'raging even to madness.' He was overstating the case, certainly, but with the worst of the Parisian Terrors making the news almost weekly, it is easy to see how the British establishment was nervous. But Britain had ulterior motives, too. First was a wish to punish the French for their intervention in the American War of Independence. It rankled with the government, and it rankled with the Navy.

Second, under the guise of declaring war on a country for assassinating its king (an instance, if ever there was one, of the pot calling the kettle black), British trading interests saw the advantages of using the war to take possession of key French islands in the Caribbean while the American government of George Washington declared a pragmatic if

Detail from a portrait of Sarah Collingwood. Reproduced courtesy of Mrs Susan Collingwood Cameron.

Collingwood's house in Oldgate, Morpeth, photographed in 1965.

ungrateful neutrality.

Although the period of the so-called Spanish Armament meant that the British fleet was in good order, the declaration of war by France in February 1793 after the execution of King Louis XVI in January found the navy suffering from under-manning, inexperience and favouritism. Collingwood had been made flag captain to an old friend, George Bowyer, now an admiral. They were offered *Prince*, a 98-gun first-rate ship of the line – vastly bigger, more unmanageable and more prestigious than anything he had had before.

For the first time since Collingwood was a midshipman, Britain was waging war against a deadly and determined enemy whose naval power was equal to hers. Though the revolution had done terrible damage to the ranks of officers in the French fleet, her ships were universally regarded as superior in build and sailing qualities to those of the corrupt and conservative British yards. Whether her new Jacobin officers could sail and fight them was another matter. Britain divided her navy into two fleets: one to protect trade in the Atlantic and prevent invasion from France; the other to wage war in the Mediterranean by seizing key strategic possessions and reinforcing (or just forcing) relations with wavering allies.

Collingwood, stationed in Atlantic and Home waters under the ageing Lord Howe, would soon be fighting in his first major fleet action. He had been at sea on and off for 30 years, and was a highly experienced, thoroughly professional seaman and commander. He had developed a way of dealing with men that was stern and reserved, but just and humane. He loathed flogging, and although he also despised mutiny and insubordination, he would rightly blame a bad crew on poor and weak officers. A story related by Collingwood's first biographer (and son-in-law), recounts how a midshipman had once reported an old and experienced sailor for some misdemeanour. Collingwood wrote to him:

Prince, a first-rate ship of the line. This ship was far bigger than any Collingwood had managed before. He would sail on her again in 1804.

In all probability the fault was yours. But whether it were or not, I am sure it would go to your heart to see a man old enough to be your father, disgraced and punished on your account; and it will, therefore, give me a good opinion of your disposition, if, when he is brought out, you ask for his pardon.

When, after receiving this letter, the midshipman duly begged the man off his punishment, Collingwood apparently said to the sailor, though with a show of pained reluctance,

This young gentleman has pleaded so humanely for you, that in the hope that you will feel a due gratitude to him for his benevolence, I will for this time overlook your offence.

No wonder it was later said by one of his junior officers that a look of displeasure from him was worse than a dozen lashes at the gangway from another captain. These were the qualities of leadership that he possessed. Now they would be put to the test.

Collingwood on his junior officers …

'… in general they are so abominably fine, and in their conceit so wise, that they think nothing wanting to their perfection but a larger hat and a pair of boots and tassels.'

~

'It is this kind of people that cause all the accidents, the loss of ships, the dreadful expense of them, mutinies, insubordination and everything bad. They must produce a certificate that they are 21 years of age, which they generally write themselves, so that they begin with forgery, proceed with knavery, and end with perjury …'

~

'I will tell you my opinion. He is as well bred, gentlemanly a young man as can be, and I dare say an excellent fox hunter, for he seems skilful in horses, dogs, foxes and such animals. But unluckily … these are branches of knowledge not very useful at sea…'

A midshipman and an admiral in the uniforms worn after Trafalgar. (From a set of drawings in the Illustrated London News, October 1905.)

And midshipmen on Collingwood …

'And then how attentive to the health of his crew? How kind to them when sick or wounded! It would have done your hearts good, as it has often done mine, to see a roasted chicken, a basin of fresh soup, a tumbler of wine, a jug of negus, or some other nice little cordial, wending its way from his table to some poor fellow riding quarantine in the sick bay.'

~

'During upwards of the three years and a half that I was in this ship, I do not remember more than four or five men being punished at the gangway, and then so slightly that it scarcely deserved the name, for the Captain was a very humane man, and although he made great allowances for the uncontrolled eccentricities of the seamen, yet he looked after the midshipmen of his ship with the eye of one who felt it a duty to keep youth in constant employment …'

'Nelson and Collingwood, who were about as yielding as their respective anchor stocks, and who regarded a shower of shot as much as a shower of snowflakes, were as tender-hearted as two schoolgirls.'

Victory and defeat 1793-1796

The winter of 1793-4 had been spent on an unsuccessful cruise which resulted in Lord Howe being criticised for failing to find and defeat the French fleet. The home press made the fleet's return uncomfortable, for to be unfortunate in war was seen as a failure almost as serious as defeat. At least the cruise had given its commanders time to get their crews into some sort of shape. But Collingwood and Bowyer now had to transfer into *Barfleur*, another first-rate, and work up a new crew to their ways. In the meantime the French were harrying Atlantic convoys, but Howe's fleet missed the French time and again. Collingwood, as depressed by the general situation as any other officer, looked to letters and news from the north for his comfort. Bounce's experience of this time is sadly unrecorded.

Howe's duties in the Atlantic, apart from hoping the French fleet would fall into his lap, included the escort of British merchant convoys to America, and the interception of convoys trading between America and France. Intelligence brought him news in spring 1794 that a convoy of 117 ships was on its way to France, and that the French fleet would be sent out to meet it. While withdrawing his frigates from Brest to allow the French to get out, Howe cruised the shipping lanes of the North Atlantic, hoping to sight and trail the convoy. When the French fleet was finally sighted, it lay between the British ships and the convoy. During three days of skirmishes Howe manoeuvred his fleet into a position of strategic advantage.

A fleet action was quite unlike anything that a frigate was likely to encounter. For one thing, line-of-battle ships were

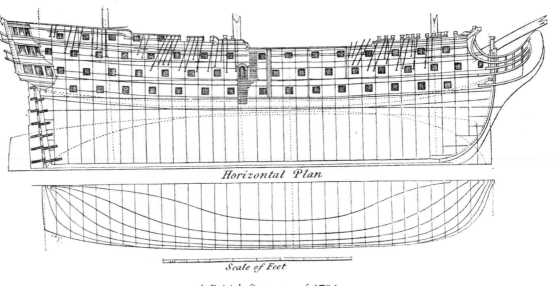

Horizontal Plan

Scale of Feet

A British first-rate of 1794.

vastly bigger: a crew of 800 or so men and officers; up to 50 guns on either side and a broadside weight of over 1000 pounds: 10 times the firepower of a 28-gun frigate. Sails, masts, rigging were more complicated and heavier to handle, and the ship harder to manoeuvre. There were three gun decks to manage, and it was paramount for discipline to be tight; at battle stations marines would be posted on every gangway to ensure that no sailor could flee his station in a moment of panic. Conditions below deck were naturally more crowded, and in battle the confusion caused by smoke, dismounted guns, people running here and there, injuries and debris may be imagined. Precision and practice in the art of gunnery was vital to gain an advantage over an enemy that might be superior in

numbers. Nelson, Collingwood, and many other captains of their generation had honed a theory and practice of gunnery excellence that, above all other considerations, would ensure a series of stunning victories over Spain and France over the next 20 years.

This was to be the largest fleet action for nearly two generations: 25 ships of the line against 25. On June 1st the battle began in earnest, each British ship choosing a French counterpart to attack in the line of battle…

…then down we went [wrote Collingwood to his father-in-law] **under a crowd of sail, and in a manner that would have animated the coldest heart, and struck terror into the most intrepid enemy. The ship we were to engage was two** ahead of the French admiral, so that we had to go through his fire, and that of the two ships next to him, and received all their broadsides two or three times before we fired a gun. I observed to the Admiral, that about that time our wives were going to church, but that I thought the peal we should ring about the Frenchman's ears would outdo their parish bells. We got very near indeed, and then began such a fire as would have done you good to have heard.

Collingwood from that moment literally had his arms full, for he caught his wounded admiral (Bowyer lost a leg) as he fell, thinking he might end up being the only officer left on deck, so fierce was the fighting. One French ship sank, and six others were taken or destroyed, while several of the

British fleet suffered severe damage.

The precious convoy had got through, so in a sense the victory was incomplete, but it was what the British public had been waiting for, and the King proclaimed it The Glorious First of June. Collingwood might be satisfied that for the second time he had behaved with courage and coolness in battle, despite the disappointment of not receiving a glorious wound. But injury he did suffer, of another sort, and it would pain him for years afterwards. It was a wound to his professional pride, and to his honour. No man's conduct on that day, it was agreed by all who had taken part, stood out: all had been brave, intelligent and equally deserving of the glory. But, after the official despatch was written to inform the Admiralty of the victory, a second letter (drafted by Sir Roger Curtis and carelessly approved by Howe) was sent in which some of the captains were singled out for praise. By implication the others were not so deserving, and Collingwood was one of them:

> The appearance of that letter had nearly broke my heart… I told Sr Roger that I considered the conduct of the Barfleur had merited commendation when commendation was given to zeal and activity and that an insinuation that either had been wanting was injurious and unjust… Lord Howe is less blamed for his letter than his Captain, who has ever been an artful, sneeking creature, whose fawning, insinuating manners creeps into the confidence of whoever he attacks… The letter… may be considered as a libel on the fleet.

Whilst those mentioned in the despatch received specially struck medals from the King, Collingwood did not. Even

1st of June

HOWE

LORD HOWE.

those who had medals felt ashamed to receive them in the furore which followed. However, Collingwood, in the eyes of those who counted, his fellow captains (Curtis aside) had distinguished himself in his first fleet action. The episode shows a marked characteristic in him: that while he took a singular lack of interest in public fame (unlike his best friend), he was very jealous indeed of his professional reputation. From now on, he was determined to bring the French to action again, in order to wipe the perceived slur from his name.

Collingwood could hardly wait for another chance to get at them and erase what he thought of as the stain on his record. In the late summer of 1794 he had a chance to go home for a little while, but spent just two days in Northumberland before having to go back to Portsmouth. His new ship *Hector*, of 74 guns, had been given to him by Lord Chatham, the First Lord of the Admiralty, who was an admirer of his; but it proved impossible to find enough men to give her a full complement, so after another brief trip home Collingwood took command of *Excellent*, also a 74, and at the beginning of 1795 shepherded a convoy of merchant vessels into the Mediterranean, where he had not sailed for nearly 25 years. Nelson, already stationed there and charged with strangling French trade, was delighted.

In between spells of blockade duty in the waters off Toulon (nicknamed Toolong by British sailors) Collingwood spent much of his time at Corsica. Corsica had been fought over for centuries, but had proved more of a burden than an asset to its many conquerors. Almost alone among the larger Mediterranean islands it remained, even at the beginning of the 19th century, a country of almost prehistoric primitiveness, wild and rugged and difficult to travel across. Corsica is also famous as the birthplace of Napoleon Bonaparte, whose

The rugged island of Corsica. Collingwood was stationed at St Florent on the north-west coast in 1795-6.

family owned a townhouse – which can still be visited – in Ajaccio, in the south-west of the island. His ambitions were far too large to be accommodated by such an insignificant backwater, and after his rise to fame in France he seems barely to have given it a thought. Collingwood had first visited Corsica in the 1760s when he was serving as a midshipman in the frigate *Gibraltar*. All we know of this visit is that, probably as a result of some injudicious dockside behaviour, three seamen belonging to the ship were stabbed to death by persons unknown. It seems to have traumatised Collingwood, then around 20 years old, and coloured his view of Corsica, as well it might.

So why had the British returned to the island? The military situation in Europe was bleak. A young Napoleon Bonaparte was destroying the finest armies that the European powers could throw at him, and Britain had no allies in the Mediterranean on whom she could rely. After the revolution of 1789 Corsica had gradually tried to reassert her independence from the French, and the resistance leader Pasquale Paoli realised that in Britain Corsica could make a powerful ally. Thus the Anglo-Corsican kingdom was born.

The French, however, were not prepared to give the island up without a fight: the island's location meant that whoever held it could blockade the French naval base at Toulon, and control trade in the whole of the western Mediterranean. Thus it came about that in 1793-4 a fleet was despatched with an army to take the island for the British. Though a

A map of Europe during the Napoleonic Wars from Hewson Clarke's History of the War, 1816.

blockade might have proved more effective in the long term, Nelson's impatience led to an attack on Calvi which cost the lives of two thirds of the British force, and during which he lost his eye. Another casualty of the aftermath of this attack was James Moutray (Mary Moutray's son), one of Nelson's

lieutenants, who died of fever.

Collingwood was stationed in St Florent with Sir John Jervis's fleet during 1795 and 1796, while relations between Paoli and the British viceroy, Sir Gilbert Elliot, deteriorated to the point of open hostility. The British made as much use of the ports and resources of the island as they could – ship repairs were easily carried out at Calvi and St Florent, and the island's famously tall and abundant pine trees were perfect for masts and spars. But Collingwood felt the island was not worth the cost in money and lives, and that the people were ungovernable.

In modern parlance, the British did not have an exit strategy, and they were at constant risk from bandits and French infiltrators – this was the period of Napoleon's lightning campaigns in Italy and many partisans began to believe that in the British they had been backing the wrong horse. At one point Collingwood complained that some local carpenters from Ajaccio who had been sacked for incompetence had taken a pot shot at the navy commissioner, a man who gloried in the name of Coffin. It got messier by the week. In October 1796 Nelson tried to cross the mountains from Bastia to St Florent, only to find that rebels had taken the heights. By the 19th he had embarked the fleet and all other British personnel and weighed anchor, having spiked the guns of the fort at Bastia, but he was bound in the bay by a gale, while the citizens tried desperately to un-spike the guns. That night, finally at sea, they by sheer luck missed the Spanish fleet sent to intercept them.

Collingwood also had a close shave in St Florent, where he and the other captains were required by Jervis to destroy batteries, forts and the Mortella Tower, and had to threaten to destroy the town before finally getting away two weeks later, whilst constantly harassed by fire from the shore. So it was that Collingwood, and the British, abandoned Corsica and the Mediterranean to the French thinking, probably, that they would never return. Ironically, the Mortella, which had caused the fleet such a nuisance, was used as a model for the

Napoleon Bonaparte. A contemporary engraving from a painting by Isabey. His spectre terrified children for a generation.

Duke of York's Martello Towers, of which 70 were built some ten years later, to defend the south coast of England from invasion by Napoleon.

Collingwood on the French …

'In their best days they were ever a set of fawning, dancing, impious hypocrites.'

~

'A Frenchman is such a trickish animal that I cannot consider him but with suspicion, and a Corsican has given proof that he can out-trick a Frenchman.'

~

'I think in the course of next month Bonaparte's experiment of the invasion will be made, and I only hope it will not be held too lightly; in that consists the only danger. They should not only be repulsed, but it should be with such exemplary vengeance as may deter them from any future attempt to subjugate our country. We should give an example to all nations how to preserve their independence.'

~

'I have a habit of not believing a Frenchman, especially when he speaks humbly of his own powers or ability, and augur well from this account of their distress'd state that something is nearly ready for execution.'

and on Napoleon in particular …

'Wherever Buonaparte reigns, there is the domination of power, which is felt or dreaded by all. His rule is repugnant to the interests and welfare of the people; and whenever his tide of greatness be at the full, his ebb will be more rapid than his rise. I cannot help thinking that epoch is not distant. In that event, the world may hope for peace for a few years, until ease and wealth make them licentious and insolent, and then our grand-children may begin the battle again.'

The execution of Louis XVI in 1792 horrified the British who were determined that the terrors of the French Revolution should not spread to England.

The Admiral.
Lord Cuthbert Collingwood, painted by William Owen c.1810.

The enemy.
Napoleon's statue surveys his birthplace, Ajaccio, Corsica.

Week & Month Days	Winds	Remarks in Funchal road, Madeira.
March 1773		Light breezes and fair weather; P.M.
	ESE	steered and set up all the rigging; Emp^d
Saturday 27th		making points, rope bands &c. received some
	East	wine on board for the ship's company.
		fired the evening and morning guns.
	East	First part moderate, latter fresh gales and
Sunday 28th		fair weather; A.M. compleated the water,
	SE	which was brought off in boats of the country
	SE^y	First part fresh breezes and cloudy with
		showers of rain, latter light airs and fair
Monday 29th	Calm	A.M. unmoored ship and hove into ½ a
		cable on the best bower.
	West	Ship's draught of water { 20..3 Abaft / 18..7 Forward

The young Cuthbert Collingwood kept meticulous logs of his voyages.
Left: in March 1773 he arrived in Madeira in HMS Portland and drew this picture of Funchal harbour. Reproduced courtesy of Mrs Susan Collingwood Cameron.

Looking towards Charlestown from Boston Harbour with USS Constitution in the foreground, the oldest floating warship in the world. Behind is the Bunker's Hill monument where the battle was fought on 17th June 1775. During the battle Collingwood showed his bravery under fire ferrying British troops across the Charles River.

English Harbour, Antigua: the entrance, Fort Berkeley and Shirley Heights.
Top right: one of the cannon dating from Collingwood's time looking out over the bay at Fort Berkeley.

Right, a portrait of Mary Moutray by John Downing. Collingwood wrote to Mary throughout his life, and one can speculate that if she had been widowed earlier, she might have become either Lady Collingwood or Lady Nelson.

Sarah Collingwood. This miniature might have accompanied Collingwood on his travels.

Above: the citadel of St Florent, north-west Corsica.

Right: the Mortella Tower at St Florent which was blown up by Collingwood in 1795.
Its design was copied, and its name adapted, by the English for the Martello Towers, 70 of which were built along the south-east coast ten years later as a defence against invasion by Napoleon.

The Battle of Cape St Vincent 14th February 1797, by J.W. Carmichael. It was here that Collingwood saved Nelson's life, but Nelson received all the public acclaim for the victory.

The eagle on the watch.

Left. Collingwood's night glass.
The Admiral 'would rise, from time to
time, to sweep the horizon with his night
glass, lest the enemy should escape in the
dark.' This night glass, a telescope with
low magnification but a huge light-
gathering lens, is preserved in the
Discovery Museum in Newcastle.

Below: Collingwood's much repaired
telescope. It was probably used at
Trafalgar. Its lenses are crusted with salt
from seaspray.

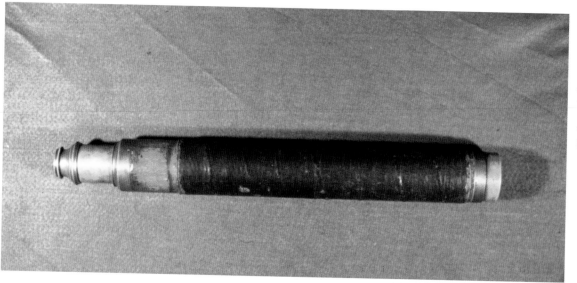

A detail from The Storm after the Battle of Trafalgar, 21st October 1805, as depicted in a painting attributed to J.W. Carmichael.

La Palazzina Cinese, Palermo. It was here that Collingwood reluctantly dined with the King of Sicily and discussed gardening. He must have been amused by the elaborate dining arrangements which included a circular table with a central section attached to a piston that rose from up the kitchen laden with food.

Right: Collingwood House, Mahon, Menorca, where Collingwood may have lived in 1809. It is now a hotel, where every week during the summer the owner gives a talk about the Admiral.

Below: Mahon today, with the old British naval base in the foreground. Collingwood has been more famous here than in his own country.

Collingwood's monument by John Graham Lough looks out to sea at Tynemouth. The Portland stone statue was installed in August 1845 by public subscription. The pedestal is by John Dobson. The four cannon, taken from Collingwood's flagship Royal Sovereign, were the first guns to fire at Trafalgar.

War and peace 1797-1802

The War now entered a critical phase. Britain had lost the Mediterranean, and France's strategy moved from defence to attack. During the winter of 1796-7 she made an abortive attempt to invade Ireland with a small fleet, intending to stir up the independence movement there. Both Spain and the Netherlands were now her allies – unwilling, but with enough naval power to stretch British resources in the Atlantic and North Sea to their limits. A French fleet of 30 sail of the line sheltered in Brest harbour while troop transports prepared for an invasion across the Channel.

At Lisbon, Sir John Jervis commanded a fleet ravaged by winter weather, leaving him just 15 ships of the line. Though severely reduced, it contained some of the best officers and ships in the navy: Waldegrave, Parker, Troubridge, Nelson in *Captain* and Collingwood in *Excellent*. Jervis – in the 30-year-old flagship *Victory* – was a hard and exacting man, but he thoroughly understood his business, and his officers respected him. So when, on 14th February 1797 – St Valentine's Day – this small fleet came across a Spanish force of 28 ships of the line, there was no question of British withdrawal.

It was Nelson's genius that when he saw an opportunity, he did not wait for permission to seize it, as Collingwood later put it:

Without much previous preparation or plan he has the faculty of discovering advantages as they arise, and the good judgement to turn them to his use. An enemy that commits a false step in his view is ruined, and it comes on him with an impetuosity that allows [them] no time to recover.

Here Nelson saw that if, as Jervis had ordered, the whole British line came about in order, they would come up with the Spanish too late; so he left the line and wearing his ship (i.e. turning it round with the wind, as opposed to tacking) went straight for them. He was soon in trouble in the general, confused melée. *Captain* became unmanageable, but she was given running repairs and carried on, covered by Collingwood and Troubridge. Collingwood forced two ships to surrender, then noticing that Nelson was again in trouble, this time against *San Nicholas*, an 80-gun ship and *San Josef* of 112 guns, ranged up to help him, at one point fighting both sides of his ship at once in a furious exchange of gunfire that was typical of Collingwood's determination and bravery. It was Nelson's character and luck to turn this sort of deadly situation to his advantage. When he saw that the two Spanish ships had fallen foul of each other, he boarded first one, then carried on across her deck and boarded the other, leading his men in a manoeuvre that delighted the British public and was dubbed Nelson's Patent Bridge.

Nelson, his own best publicist, wrote a colourful account

of this exploit which earned him instant immortality at home but, ever generous to his friends, he also gave Collingwood a ringing endorsement:

... Captain Collingwood, disdaining the parade of taking possession of beaten enemies, most gallantly pushed up, with every sail set, to save his old friend and mess-mate, who was to appearance in a critical state.

And to Collingwood himself he wrote:

My dearest friend, 'A friend in need is a friend indeed' was never more truly verified than by your most noble and gallant conduct yesterday in sparing the Captain from further loss; and I beg, both as a public officer and a friend, you will accept my most sincere thanks.

It had been a bloody and desperate affair, with a long butcher's bill of killed and wounded. The British, outnumbered two to one, had taken four ships of the line (all of them victims of Collingwood's shattering broadsides) and mauled many more. They had also proved that British gunnery was so vastly superior to that of the Spanish that they could always count on being able to attack a much larger enemy with confidence. The action was named after the cape off which it was fought, and Jervis was given an earldom of the same name: St Vincent. Nelson was promoted to Rear Admiral and made a Knight of the Bath. This time, all the captains were praised (there was a universally high opinion of Collingwood's conduct from his fellow officers). This time too all the captains were awarded medals by the king. Collingwood, determined not to forget the pain of The

Glorious First of June, refused his, saying that if he deserved one now, he had deserved one then. Jervis, knowing Collingwood very well and expecting just such a refusal, had already arranged that he would also be presented with the medal for the First of June, and so Collingwood, uniquely in 1797, was presented with two medals. The slight was erased, and Collingwood, satisfied with the respect and honour of his peers, desired that his letters home concerning the action should not be shown around, as it might look as if he was showing off.

Collingwood kept another souvenir of the battle: a 50lb doubled-headed bar-shot from the huge Spanish flagship *Santissima Trinidada* (130 guns) which flew across his quarterdeck and expended itself against the foot of *Excellent*'s mainmast. Collingwood sent it as a gift to his father-in-law with a note to the effect that these things were not much fun when they flew about one's head. This brutal-looking reminder of the personal danger faced by sailors is still in the possession of the Blackett family.

It remains a mystery that two such men as Collingwood and Nelson, in so many ways opposites of each other, should forge and maintain such a loyal and warm friendship over so long a period. Collingwood was reserved, though he had a temper; found it difficult to make friends, and maintained a distance between himself and his men that was sometimes resented, and often unfavourably compared to his friend's rash, passionate relationships, quick to grow and sometimes equally quick to die in an outburst of jealousy and hurt.

Nelson, though not a humorist like Collingwood, had fire in him. In many ways immature, certainly vain and self-promoting, hypochondriacal and frequently depressive – and an undisputed genius of naval command – he nevertheless

Ships battle at sea.

Nelson, as depicted in William James' Naval History, 1837.

Collingwood, from the same book.

shared with Collingwood a deep and abiding love for his country, matched by a hatred of the French and their revolution. They both cared very much about the naval service: its ships and men, its honour and success. Collingwood saw in him heroism on a grand scale and admired the devotion he inspired. Nelson in turn loved Collingwood for his cool bravery, his unstoppable determination, and the supreme excellence of his seamanship, management and sense of justice.

Both men, along with all their fellow captains, were horrified, furious and wretchedly sad when news circulated in the fleet of a mutiny in the spring of 1797. They had been away from England for four years. In 1795 there had been bread riots at home caused by a shortage of grain, the King's carriage had been stoned by an angry mob, and fears of a French-style revolution, terrors and all, spreading to England created extraordinary tension, to which the fleet was not immune. But the main cause of the mutinies seems to have been a genuine set of grievances. The most obvious was that the pay of a seaman in the navy had not risen since the days of Charles II, more than 100 years previously; but there were others. In fact, the first mutiny, at Spithead on Easter Sunday, was more of a strike in our modern terms. A petition was presented, very politely, without threat of violence. Admiral Howe, well-respected by the seamen, went to pacify them, and agreed to the bulk of their demands. The mutiny ended, and the fleet put to sea.

Far more serious was a mutiny which broke out at the Nore (a sandbank in the Thames estuary near the mouth of the River Medway) on May 12th. It was led by Richard Parker of the 98-gun *Sandwich*, and soon spread through Admiral Duncan's fleet, watching the Dutch coast for an expected invasion fleet. At the end of June it was suppressed by a combination of force and cajoling: Parker and 24 other mutineers were hanged at the yardarm. By October, Duncan had sufficient control of the fleet to meet the Dutch at Camperdown in a bloody but brilliant victory which resulted in more than 1000 casualties on both sides, and the capture of seven ships of the line by the British.

Jervis meanwhile recommended that any hard nuts in the fleet be sent to Collingwood, so that he could 'bring them to order'. The records of most of his ships' logs – Collingwood was one of the first to keep an accurate record of punishments – show how little he resorted to physical punishment compared with other captains like Nelson and Hardy; three or four floggings in a year, sometimes. Instead, he would stop grog rations and dole out unpopular, humiliating jobs – there was never any shortage of these on a three-decker ship of the line – relying on the peer-pressure of the lower decks to flush out any seditious thoughts. The exceptions to this, perhaps, were the beatings he gave midshipmen – and they were grateful that he walloped them in the privacy of the great cabin, rather than in front of the men.

While Collingwood suffered the boredom of convoy duty, Nelson was sent to Teneriffe to intercept a treasure ship

The mutiny on the Nore. Richard Parker, President of the Committee of Delegates, tendering the list of grievances to Vice-Admiral Buckner on board the Sandwich.

expected from the Americas. In perhaps his most disastrous action, Nelson launched an assault on the island when he knew the element of surprise had already been lost. An appalling list of casualties included Nelson himself, who lost an arm to go with the eye he had sacrificed at Calvi.

The year 1798 was another of mixed fortunes. Napoleon, now undisputed military master of France, embarked on his infamous Egyptian expedition, not merely to control Egypt, but to force a route through to the Red Sea and ultimately to threaten India. There was rebellion in Ireland, brutally put down.

Morpeth Market Place in the early 19th century.

Collingwood was still stuck on blockade duty, disappointed that Nelson, recovered from his wounds and depression, was sent without him into the Mediterranean to track down and destroy Napoleon's invasion fleet. So it was that he missed, in August 1798, the Battle of the Nile, in which a substantial part of the French fleet was destroyed by a combination of brilliant British tactics and French ineptitude. At home, and throughout the fleet, there was rejoicing: an 'illumination' took place at Newcastle on October 5th to celebrate the victory, and Collingwood rejoiced too in his comrade's glory.

Collingwood was by now desperate to go home, having been continuously at sea since 1793. In December 1798 *Excellent* was finally ordered to return to Spithead and pay off her crew. Cuthbert was reunited with a wife whose separation from him had been twice as long as their marriage. And when one talks of the hardship of naval life during this period, it seems nothing was harder for men like Collingwood than these years of estrangement. His daughters did not recognise him, though he was by now famous enough to be received everywhere with warmth and admiration. While he was in Morpeth he also finally received promotion to the rank of Rear Admiral of the White (second lowest of nine ranks of Admiral), and when he was in London briefly in March, he was presented to the King and Queen at a 'drawing room'. Unlike Nelson, Collingwood was unimpressed by the aura of monarchy, and he thought the etiquette of the court fatuous and meaningless.

It was an entertaining sight, to so new a courtier, to observe the pleasure that sprang into the countenances of all, when her Majesty was graciously pleased to repeat to them a few words which were not intended to have any meaning; for the great art of the courtly manner seems to be to smile on all, to speak of all, and yet leave no trace of meaning in what is said.

For all his delight at returning to Morpeth, Collingwood was so concerned with the state of the war that he applied for a new ship. There were rumours of a shore posting, but he wrote to a friend that he had 'no desire to command in a port, except at Morpeth, where I am only second'. In May 1799 he was given command – the first time he had hoisted his admiral's flag – of a 74 gun ship, *Triumph*, a slow two-decker, even older than *Victory*, which he found in a deplorable state.

For the first time he had to deal with having a captain under him on his ship. It was not a happy relationship:

I have a captain here (Stephens), a very novice in the conduct of fleets or ships. When I joined her I found she had been twice ashore, and once on fire, in the three months he had commanded her, and they were then expecting that the ships company should mutiny every day. I never saw men more orderly, or who seem better disposed, but I suppose they took liberties when they found they might, and I am afraid there are a great many ships where the reigns of discipline are held very loosely, the effect of a long war and an overgrown navy.

Collingwood sorted both men and officers out quickly.

But the commission was unsuccessful. Following rumours that the French were planning an invasion of Menorca, the fleet went into the Mediterranean, found on arriving at Port Mahon that the rumours were false, and chased the French fleet all the way back to Brest at the mouth of the English Channel. It returned to England with nothing to show for its efforts – an episode which summed up the last two years of the war for Collingwood.

Napoleon now returned from Egypt, overthrew the ruling Directory and established himself as First Consul. Within seven months he would meet the Austrian army at Marengo and defeat them. Nothing, it seemed, could halt the tide of his ambition. Like everyone else, Collingwood was torn between horror and a commander's respect for genius…

Is it not wonderful that this young man Bonaparte, without that experience which has been thought necessary to the command of great armies, is able to defeat all the schemes and armies that the best Austrian officers can present to him?

A new century began. In London, the first soup kitchens were set up to relieve the hungry poor in a freezing January. Josiah Spode was perfecting his technique for making bone china, and the Royal Institution for applied science was founded. An Act of Union was passed between Britain and Ireland. In May, James Hadfield fired a shot at King George III at the Theatre Royal in Drury Lane. And within a year, Richard Trevithick would be demonstrating his steam passenger carriage. The modern world was dawning.

For Collingwood the new century began with frustrations. Throughout 1800 he was stationed in the West country, at Torbay or Cawsand Bay near Plymouth. He raised his flag in *Barfleur*, the grand and spacious 98 gun three-decker in which he had been flag captain at the Glorious First of June. This was a time of short cruises in the Channel, with the constant fear that Napoleon would launch another invasion of Ireland. And the often terrible weather took its toll on both ships and men. Collingwood was becoming grumpier and more short-tempered, though his strong will prevented him from showing it to his men. He had been ill, too, with a bowel complaint – cured by wearing a flannel waistcoat – compounded by insomnia

Sarah's long journey from Morpeth to Plymouth in January 1801, with eight-year-old Sal, involved three cramped days in an uncomfortable coach.

and depression. These were caused by boredom, lack of exercise and the constant strain of command. Collingwood was notoriously bad at delegating, conducting business by himself that a modern manager would off-load on to a bevy of underlings.

Meanwhile, there were rumours that secret negotiations were going on between Britain and France to bring about a peace settlement that everyone was desperate for. The thought made Collingwood long for home – Sarah was in the process of buying the house in Morpeth – where he could stroll in his garden along what he called his quarterdeck walk, plant vegetables and trees, and oversee the education of his daughters. But the war dragged on in desultory fashion through the winter and beyond, into 1801.

Collingwood decided he could wait no longer for the joys of the conjugal embrace. So in mid-January, at the worst possible time of year, Sarah set off from Morpeth on the long, uncomfortable journey to Plymouth, bringing with her little

Sal – now eight – and leaving Mary Patience behind in the care of various aunts. Collingwood's account of her arrival paints a vivid and poignant scene:

I had been reckoning on the possibility of her arrival that Tuesday, when about two o'clock I received an express to go to sea immediately with all the ships that were ready; and had we not then been engaged at a court-martial, I might have got out that day: but this business delayed me until near night, and I determined to wait on shore until eight o'clock for the chance of their arrival. I went to dine with Lord Nelson; and while we were at dinner their arrival was announced to me. I flew to the inn where I had desired my wife to come, and found her and little Sarah as well after their journey as if it had lasted only for the day. No greater happiness is human nature capable of than was mine that evening; but at dawn we parted, and I went to sea…

... as did Nelson, shortly afterwards, on a mission to the Baltic, where the government had decided that strong-arm tactics were required to prevent Denmark, Sweden and Russia making common cause with the French during peace negotiations. Nelson was junior commander to Sir Hyde Parker, a weak, dilatory man. In the furious battle that Nelson narrowly won at Copenhagen in April, Parker merely stood by and made his infamous signal to disengage, equally famously ignored by Nelson. Nelson's life was now much less harmonious than Collingwood's. He had finally split with the unhappy Fanny after his scandalous affair with Emma Hamilton, and as a result been deliberately snubbed not just by service colleagues, but even by the King himself. The victory at Copenhagen, though reinforcing his fame and glory in the eyes of the British public, brought him no nearer to his own inner peace.

Collingwood never openly criticised his friend for what he called his 'attachment' – he was far too loyal and knew his friend too well. But it must have given him cause for grief as it did many of Nelson's friends, to see how easily his head had been turned by the ersatz glamour of the Neapolitan court and the charms of a manipulative, ambitious woman. Collingwood also had his doubts about the impending peace, for he thought it possible – and in the long run he was right – that it might prove illusory. He was more convinced by June 1802 when, finally, the Treaty of Amiens was signed, and he could at last go home to Morpeth:

I am sure I have had my share of the war. I begun it early and see the last of it, and I hope it is the last we shall ever see.

The peace lasted 14 months.

Peace and war 1803-1804

Collingwood was at home again in Morpeth, writing to his friends as if he had never left home:

I should recommend Northumberland for your residence, a fine healthy air; in winter a comfortable fire and friends about you that would be made happy by your neighbourhood.

His preferred employment now was reading history, the education of his daughters whom he barely knew, and the cultivation of his garden. His son-in-law recalled that on one occasion,

A brother admiral, who had sought him in the garden in vain, at last discovered him with his gardener, old Scott, to whom he was much attached, in the bottom of a deep trench, which they were busily occupied in digging.

He had a busy social life too, catching up on family, friends and old acquaintances he had not seen for three years. And the family found time towards the end of the summer to go to the seaside at Newbiggin, where bathing cured all their colds and other minor ailments. Mary Patience, the youngest, had got over the measles and Sal was hoping to catch it soon. Both were very diligent in their lessons. However, war was

Collingwood's longed-for garden at Morpeth with his 'quarterdeck walk', photographed in 1936.

looming again, and Collingwood's contacts with government and the Admiralty gave him ample warning of it. While France was busy preparing for the next phase of the conflict, England's peace dividend from the treaty

> On Saturday last, Admiral Collingwood passed through this place on his way to the admiralty to take a command. The corporation of this town, in compliment to this gallant officer, have offered an additional bounty of one guinea to each seaman entering to serve in his ship.

On 28th May 1803 Newcastle Courant reported that Collingwood had passed through the town. It was to be the last time he saw his home.

was the chance to stand down much of her expensive army and navy. Under the terms of the treaty she agreed to give up Malta on condition that its neutrality would be respected. Britain now saw that if she left the island it would immediately be taken by the French, and that left unchecked Bonaparte would soon once again seize control of the Mediterranean. And so it was that in May 1803 Britain withdrew her ambassador from Paris, and declared war on the old enemy.

The country was soon awash with rumours that Napoleon was planning an invasion of England, as indeed he was. In Newcastle in June a 'loyal armed association', 1200 men strong, was sworn in. In August they marched to the Town Moor in ten companies, and received their muskets. There was a huge commotion across the region when beacon fires, standing ready in case of invasion, were accidentally lit, causing widespread panic. Collingwood received a letter from the Admiralty asking if he was ready to go to sea at short notice. 'I answered, "to be sure I was", and packed up my trunk and my signal book, and am now waiting for a summons to take my station wherever it may be.'

By July 1803 he was at sea again, having unwittingly said goodbye to Morpeth, Sarah and his girls for the last time. He

was given command of *Venerable*, a 74-gun two-decker, and ordered to join Cornwallis on the Brest blockade. Guarding the mouth of the English Channel against invasion through the winter months must have been the worst job in the navy. To add to the miserable discomfort of Atlantic gales, and the tension of knowing that Bonaparte's 130,000 strong Army of England was poised to capitalise on any tactical errors, was the sailor's greatest horror: a lee-shore. In order to blockade the French Channel fleet in Brest effectively, the English fleet had to stay as close to the coast as possible, but relentless south-westerly winds that forced them into treacherous coastal waters with their outlying rocks and wicked tidal streams meant constant danger of shipwreck.

Collingwood's misery was compounded: he sailed *Venerable* out in such a hurry to join Cornwallis that he forgot to bring a spare coat. But, forever bearing the burden of responsibility, he confined his complaints to letters home. It was a station, he wrote,

Of great anxiety and required a constant care and look out… I have often been a whole week without having my clothes off, and sometimes up on deck the whole night. I was there longer than intended for want of a proper successor, and saw all my squadron relieved more than once. The Newcastle volunteers, with the two youngsters, joined about a fortnight since; they are a set of stout young men and a great addition to my strength…

Now was the time of greatest danger, and Collingwood was convinced that the blow would fall very soon. Frequently, he and his trusted lieutenant, John Clavell, would sleep together on deck on a gun, from which the Admiral 'would rise, from time to time, to sweep the horizon with his night glass, lest the enemy should escape in the dark.' This night glass, a telescope with low magnification but a huge light-gathering lens, is preserved in the Discovery Museum in Newcastle.

In December Collingwood was in Plymouth, sheltering from storms that had destroyed several ships in the Channel. He then transferred to *Culloden*, another 74, and a veteran of the battles of the Glorious First of June, Cape St Vincent and the Nile.

All through that winter the fleet's frigates were employed in harrying French invasion forces in their harbours along the Channel coast, causing more irritation than harm but exciting the British press to some effect. Fear at home had precipitated political upheaval at the heart of government: in the spring of 1804 William Pitt replaced Henry Addington as Prime Minister, and St Vincent was removed from the Admiralty.

Collingwood's short time in *Culloden* – three months – was unremarkable, though he was given his promotion to Vice-Admiral of the Blue. Now he was back cruising off Ushant, his thoughts strayed to Northumberland, where he hoped his girls were being 'virtuously educated'. And even with his many cares, he had time to feel for a fellow Geordie, a nurseryman from 'Wrighton' (Ryton), who had been pressed into the navy on the grounds that he had once been to sea when he was young:

'They have broken up his good business at home, distressed his family, and sent him here, where he is of little or no service. I grieve for him, poor man!'

This caricature of a press gang at work was published in 1782.

Still the invasion did not come. Bonaparte, perhaps, was busy: he had just had himself crowned Emperor of France: 'as much villainy as ever disgraced nature in the person of one man,' was Collingwood's verdict. But prospects of an end to the war were bleak. England apart, there was no power in Europe to compete with the new empire: 'Russia cannot; Prussia will not; Austria dare not. All the rest must do as they are ordered', wrote Collingwood. All the rest included Spain, whose passive aid to France was becoming active, and against whom Britain declared war too.

Brest and the mouth of the English Channel. Bonaparte was poised to invade.

Collingwood, meanwhile, had changed ships again. After a brief spell in *Prince*, the 98-gun first-rate in which he had been flag captain in 1793, he was given *Dreadnought*, another three-decker, which he immediately liked, though he complained that as a result of St Vincent's 'savings' she had been fitted out by unqualified contractors and needed a great deal of work to set her right. Nevertheless, within a year he had worked her crew up to such a pitch of perfection, that she recorded the fastest rate of broadside firing that the navy had ever seen. Collingwood's view, shared by Nelson and others of their persuasion, was that to defeat the enemy the fleet must bring overwhelming firepower to bear: faster, more accurate, more determined and more prolonged. No enemy could compete with the staggering rate of three broadsides in three and a half minutes that Collingwood achieved.

The Commerce de Marseilles, a French first-rate captured at Toulon in 1792 by Admiral Hood. She carried 128 guns.
Her capture enabled improvements to be made to British ships. French ships were more suited to Mediterranean sailing than British ships
which were built to brave the bigger seas of the Atlantic and were not so manoeuvrable.

Trafalgar 1805: 'that noble fellow ...'

The situation in Europe was as bleak as it had ever been. Napoleon's mastery of the continent would continue for many more years. Where the new Emperor was vulnerable was at sea. The most brilliant general since Julius Caesar, Napoleon was able to calculate military strategy with great precision, but he never understood the sea, where the margin for error was always much greater. Nor did he have senior officers of the calibre of Collingwood and Nelson. He was right when he said he only needed to control the English Channel for a day to become master of Great Britain; but he underestimated how long a day could be at sea.

Throughout the early part of 1805 he watched and waited as his Army of England champed at the bit in the harbours and ports of the Channel. Orders had gone out to the fleets at Brest, Rochefort and Toulon to escape their blockades, head for the West Indies with the Spanish fleet to distract the English, rendezvous there and head back for the Channel: by a certain date. His idea was to make a landing in Ireland with overwhelming force, drawing the British forces there and leaving the Channel clear. Nelson headed after them with a squadron once their destination was known, but narrowly missed them. Collingwood stayed behind, patrolling off Cadiz, his own thoughts on the matter showing, not for the last time, that he at least had not been fooled...

... I think it is not improbable that I shall have all those fellows coming from the West Indies again, before the Hurricane months, unless they sail from thence directly for Ireland, which I have always had an idea was their plan, for this Bonoparte [sic] has as many tricks as a monkey. I believe their object in the West Indies to be less conquest, than to draw our force from home.

Nelson, frustrated by having missed Admiral Villeneuve's force in the West Indies, returned to Gibraltar, and from there he corresponded with Collingwood, who was at Cadiz keeping the returned combined fleet under surveillance. They were of the same mind, straining all their resources – mostly frigates and what little intelligence was to be had in the Mediterranean – to anticipate the next move of the enemy. But Collingwood had an additional problem, as he complained to his sister:

I have a diligent young man for my secretary and Clavell, my lieutenant, is the spirit of the ship; but such a captain [Rotherham], such a stick, I wonder very much how such people get forward. I should (I firmly believe) with his nautical ability and knowledge and exertion, have been a bad lieutenant at this day. Was he brought up in the navy? For he has very much the stile of the Coal trade about him, except that they are good seamen.

Rotherham, a Hexham man, had indeed been brought up in the coal-trade. And although Collingwood notoriously disliked having any sort of a flag-captain under him, Rotherham does seem to have been uniquely bad at his job, as a fellow officer later recalled:

Collingwood's dry caustic mind lives before me in the recollection of his calling across the deck his fat stupid captain – long since dead – when he had seen him commit some monstrous blunder, and after the usual bowing and formality – which the excellent old chief never omitted – he said: 'Captain, I have been thinking, whilst I looked at you, how strange it is that a man should grow so big and know so little. That's all, Sir; that's all.' Hats off; low bows.

Because of the events of October 1805, the world has generally forgotten what happened on August 20th of that year. It was one of the most brilliant naval actions of the war, although hardly a gun was fired. It began when Collingwood in *Dreadnought*, with *Colossus* and *Achille* and the *Niger* (a frigate) were patrolling off Cadiz. Over the horizon that morning, just after dawn, came 26 enemy ships. Collingwood's tiny squadron lay between them and eight Spanish ships in the port. There was nothing he could do but run for it, knowing that the odds of escaping such a fleet with his slow old ships, let alone fighting them, were negligible. Two hours later 16 of the enemy's fastest ships were detached and sent after him as he made for Gibraltar.

Knowing the situation was critical, Collingwood then pulled off a masterstroke: he shortened sail, turned back, and sent the very fast *Colossus* off to get as close to the enemy as

possible, meanwhile throwing out a series of signals. The enemy saw that Collingwood must have sighted a large British force in the distance and that he had decided to wait for them and fight. So the French turned tail and fled back to Cadiz: 16 ships of the line had been seen off by three.

The stage was now set. Russia, Sweden and Austria had joined Britain in a grand coalition against France. Bonaparte had to strike soon. On the continent his target was Austria – in December he would destroy her armies at Austerlitz. Villeneuve, with 35 ships of the combined fleet, was kept under constant watch by Collingwood, now reinforced and with 26 ships. Nelson, in *Victory*, had gone back to England for a few weeks' leave while Collingwood, as ever, stuck to his duty. With summer waning towards autumn, it was now or never. Napoleon sensed that the season was too late for another invasion attempt and ordered Villeneuve to break out of Cadiz and head for the Mediterranean.

Villeneuve, depressed and having little confidence in the Combined Fleet, found excuses to stay in Cadiz. He knew his crews were no match for English sailors who had been almost constantly at sea for 12 years; he had little faith in the effectiveness of the Spanish, even with their ships' massive firepower. But at last his hand was forced: word reached him that Napoleon had sent an officer to supersede him, and that on being recalled to Paris he would feel the fury of his master's displeasure.

Nelson, meanwhile, left England for the last time, and came to take over the blockading squadron from his old friend. There were to be 'no little jealousies'. No man had 'more faith in another' than he had in his friend, and Collingwood was to be given complete freedom of action. But Nelson also played a joke on his old comrade. He had

Victory c.1780 from a contemporary engraving. By the time of Trafalgar she was considered ancient at 40 years old.

Royal Sovereign, from an engraving reproduced in the Illustrated London News, October 1905.

brought Collingwood *Royal Sovereign*, a 100-gun ship like *Victory. Royal Sovereign* was known in the service as the West Country Wagon, a notoriously slow sailer, even more so than Collingwood's dear *Dreadnought*. Was this an insult? What Collingwood did not know, until he joined her, was that she had just been freshly re-coppered, and with a smooth, gleaming hull was transformed into the fastest ship in the British fleet; although he was sad to lose a crew that were used to his ways and were perfectly ready for battle, he found his new ship to be in very good shape. He took most of his officers, and some of his men with him.

Nelson and Collingwood met again on board *Victory* where, with the other captains and admirals in the fleet, Nelson explained his plan of battle, should Villeneuve be persuaded to come out. Nelson called it, with typical immodesty, the Nelson Touch. The idea was that, facing a numeri-

cally larger fleet, the British forces would try to detach a part of the enemy from the battle and defeat the rest before they could re-join. He was counting on a conservative approach from the combined fleet. They would probably form a single line, as was traditional. Nelson would form his ships into two lines, and instead of the two fleets closing each other on parallel courses, he would have his two lines attack at nearly right angles, breaking the enemy line a third of the way from the front and rear. The vanguard of the enemy would be cut off long enough for victory to be secured before they could rejoin the battle.

This was not quite such a radical idea as has often been argued, but it had the merit of being conceived in the Nelsonian way: within the plan, each captain was free to improvise, and the crucial thing was to get as close to the enemy as quickly as possible and destroy him with accurate gunfire. There was an additional advantage: the officers and men of the British fleet knew that with Nelson leading them they could not lose. The enemy believed they could not win.

On 19th October 1805 the weather was so beautiful that Nelson sent to *Royal Sovereign* to ask if Collingwood would come over to dine. But the two friends would never see each other again. Just as Collingwood was about to reply, a signal was made that the enemy were on their way out. Villeneuve, feeling the hounds snapping at his heels, had seen an opportunity to run from Cadiz into the Mediterranean, and brought the whole fleet out under protest from the Spanish admirals. Once out, he realised that escape was impossible, and on the morning of October 21st, the two fleets – 27 British against 33 of the enemy – found themselves in light winds and a slight swell, facing each other off Cape Trafalgar. Collingwood's servant, Smith, later wrote this account of that morning:

I entered the Admiral's cabin about daylight, and found him already up and dressing. He asked if I had seen the French fleet; and on my replying that I had not, he told me to look out at them, adding that, in a very short time, we should see a great deal more of them. I then observed a crowd of ships to leeward; but I could not help looking with still greater interest at the Admiral, who, during all this time was shaving himself with a composure which quite astonished me.

Whatever 'Old Cuddy' was feeling inside, his masterly sense of self-discipline would never allow it to be shown to the men. He went up on deck to talk to his crew, reminding Clavell on the way to put on silk stockings, as these were easier for the surgeon to deal with when amputating limbs during battle. Neither he nor his fat, stupid, but undeniably brave Captain Rotherham (nor, fatally, Nelson on board *Victory*) could be persuaded to change out of their full dress uniforms.

Collingwood noticed some Newcastle men who had come over with him from *Dreadnought*, and stopped to encourage them: 'Today, my lads' he said, 'we must show those fellows what the Tars of the Tyne can do.' And then he addressed his officers: 'Now, gentlemen, let us do something today that the world may talk of hereafter.' It was now that Nelson raised his famous signal, which was supposed to read: Nelson confides that every man will do his duty. But because of the new telegraphing system of flag signals, in which some words were represented by a single flag and others had to be spelled letter by letter, it was easier to send: England expects... Collingwood said impatiently, 'I wish Nelson would stop signalling. We all know what we have to do.'

A race now developed between Nelson and Collingwood, as their ships pressed on more sail in order to be the first into battle. *Royal Sovereign* won it effortlessly. It was just before noon. A thousand yards from the French and Spanish line, *Royal Sovereign* sailed inexorably towards them. Six of the enemy opened fire on her, 32- and 50-pound shot at first falling into the sea and then, as she came closer, tearing at her sails and rigging and flinging splinters of wood around the decks with deadly effect. Often, in such circumstances, a broadside would be let off to calm the men and create a defensive pall of smoke. But Collingwood, now well ahead of *Victory* and the ships of his own line, disdained to fire, to the

Nelson on the deck of Victory just before the Battle of Trafalgar: a romanticised 19th century illustration.

great admiration of Nelson, who cried, 'See how that noble fellow, Collingwood, takes his ship into action. How I envy him!' The effect on the enemy's morale was shattering.

At last Collingwood having had the sailing master lay his ship for a point between *Fougeux* and the Spanish flagship *Santa Anna* – a vast great ship of 112 guns which towered over *Royal Sovereign* – allowed a broadside to be fired for covering smoke, and then forced *Royal Sovereign* into the rapidly closing gap. These are the very guns, incidentally, which now stand guard at Collingwood's monument at Tynemouth. As she passed through, *Royal Sovereign* fired two devastating broadsides into the stern of the *Santa Anna*, dismounting many of her guns and killing and wounding more than 100 men. The two ships then locked together and began a furious exchange of gunfire, and before any other English ship had joined the action, *Royal Sovereign* was surrounded by several more enemy ships in a deadly fight to the finish.

Collingwood, as ever, maintained his cool. A sail had fallen and lay over the gangway. He and Clavell folded it up, putting it neatly away for another day. He went up and down the upper decks encouraging his men and lending a hand wherever it was needed, while a withering fire was kept up by enemy sharpshooters. He was seen munching an apple. At some point he was injured severely in the leg by a great jagged splinter, but carried on regardless. By the end of the day he was one of only three officers left alive on his quarterdeck.

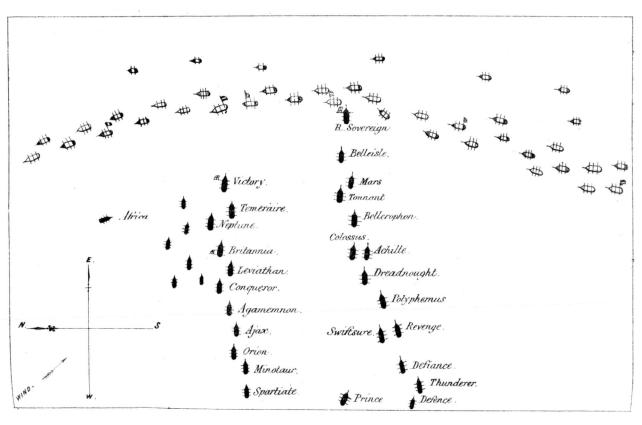

The British and combined French and Spanish fleets at noon, 21st October 1805, as recorded in Nelson's Dispatches.

The Battle of Trafalgar, left to right Euryalus, Victory, and Temeraire approach the enemy lines.

Collingwood later wrote in his dispatch about the furious battle that followed, and what happened to the Temeraire: 'The Temeraire was boarded by accident or design, by a French ship on one side and a Spaniard on the other; the contest was vigorous, but in the end the combined ensigns were torn from the poop, and the British hoisted in their places.'

After Royal Sovereign had lost her masts Collingwood boarded the Euryalus and transferred his flag to her.

At two o'clock *Santa Anna* finally surrendered to Collingwood, at which time he had word that Nelson had been wounded, and he ordered the frigate *Euryalus* to take the crippled *Royal Sovereign* under tow. Nelson was not alone. The British suffered 450 killed and over 1200 wounded. The French and Spanish took more than 7000 killed and wounded: a ratio of more than 4:1 which reflects almost exactly the rates of broadside fire: the difference in gunnery technique and training between the two fleets.

Collingwood's official journal records tersely that towards the end of the afternoon he was informed of the death of the Commander in Chief. But a seaman on *Royal Sovereign*, known to us only as Sam, gave a much more human and touching account:

Our dear Admiral Nelson is killed! So we have paid pretty sharply for licking 'em. I never sat eyes on him, for which I am both sorry and glad; for, to be sure, I should like to have seen him – but then, all the men who have seen him are such soft toads, they have done nothing but blast their eyes, and cry, ever since he was killed. God bless you! Chaps that fought like the devil, sit down and cry like a wench. I am still in the Royal Sovereign, but the Admiral has left her, for she is like a horse without a bridle, so he is on a frigate that he may be here and there and everywhere … as bold as a lion for all he can cry! – I saw his tears with my own eyes, when the boat hailed and said my lord was dead.

On the day of Trafalgar the British fleet took 17 enemy ships and sunk one, the most crushing victory that had ever been achieved in a naval battle. But the victory was not com-

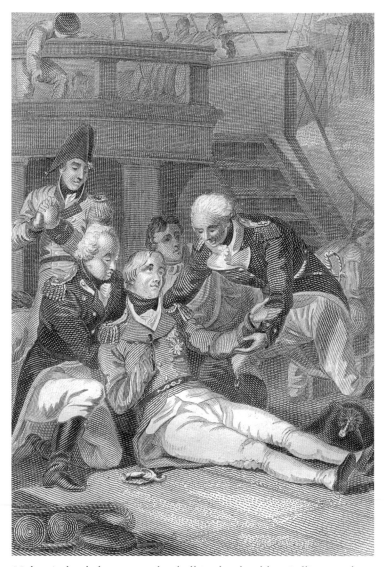

Nelson's death from a musket ball in the shoulder. Collingwood later wrote: 'I have only to lament, in common with the British navy and the British nation … the loss of a hero … but my heart is rent with the most poignant grief for the loss of a dear friend.'

plete, and would not be completed. Nelson had ordered that the fleet be anchored after the battle, but many ships were in such an appalling state that they didn't even possess anchors, and worse was to come. A terrible storm blew up from the west, lasting several days, during which many of the prizes had to be cast off – some returned to port, many were wrecked – and it was only the extraordinary skill of Collingwood and his captains that prevented a single one of the dismasted and half-wrecked British fleet from being lost. Captain Blackwood of *Euryalus*, having come to know Collingwood for the first time, reported that he found the Admiral to be 'a reserved, though a very pleasing good man, and as he fought like an angel, I take the more to him.'

It was not until November 6th that Collingwood's famous despatch, carried overland from Falmouth to London in an epic non-stop coach ride, reached the Admiralty in the small hours of a very foggy London morning. The Prime Minister was woken at 3am, the King in Windsor at 6.30. No-one knew whether to cry for joy or with grief; so they did both, as did the whole country. Just two days later, on Saturday, November 8th, the *Newcastle Courant* reported:

Providence has blessed his majesty's arms with a signal victory over the combined fleets, before Cadiz, but it has thought fit to chasten our exultations by depriving us of a man, whose very name was a tower of strength – LORD NELSON.

And a week later…

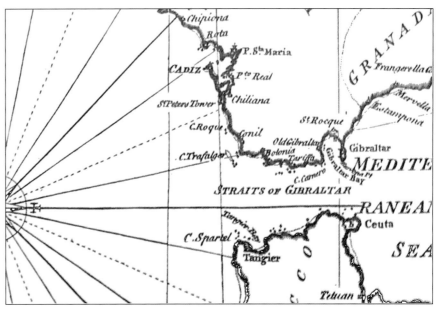

Trafalgar's vital position at the entrance to the Mediterranean.

Admiral Collingwood's conduct has obtained the fullest approbation; and despatches have been sent off, containing a commission, which appoints him to the command of the ships in the Mediterranean, with the same powers as Lord Nelson had. It will be observed in the Gazette that our gallant townsman is now Baron Collingwood of Caldburne and Hethpool in Northumberland.

Sarah Collingwood was in town shopping when she heard the news. The mail coach, draped in black, came clattering across the Tyne Bridge; the coachman shouted 'Great British victory: all the English admirals are dead!' Sarah fainted.

King of the Mediterranean 1806-1808

Cuthbert Collingwood was now famous. He was a Vice-Admiral of the Red, an hereditary peer, and what was more, he had inherited the mantle of England's Saviour from his dying comrade. He was Commander-in-Chief of the Mediterranean fleet, a position of almost vice-regal power from which he had to deal not only with the fleet – 80 men of war and sundry others – but also Britain's armies, her enemies and friends: kings, queens, deys, beys, pashas, sultans, envoys and ambassadors, and ministers by the score. King George thought his despatch from Trafalgar one of the finest things he had ever read.

This was enough to keep a young, healthy man at his post from dawn until midnight. Collingwood was now 57: his eyes were failing, his bowels caused him pain, insomnia and loss of appetite. Tied to his desk, he lacked exercise, and the constant worry and burden of command made him wish for home more than ever. A barony might have been a source of comfort to a man who sought public acclaim. Collingwood's typical reaction was less enthusiastic:

And so I have a great Barony – it may be called a Barreny to me – value 30s. a year, or thereabouts. But if I live long enough I will make it a place of consideration.

But if Collingwood was unimpressed, his men and the entire fleet bathed in the glow of reflected glory. And not just

the officers and men. As Collingwood wrote to Sarah (now Lady Collingwood), Bounce was less immune than his master to flattery…

The consequential airs he gives himself since he became a right honourable dog are insufferable. He considers it beneath his dignity to play with commoners' dogs, and truly thinks that he does them grace when he condescends to lift up his leg against them. This, I think, is carrying the insolence of rank to the extreme, but he is a dog that does it.

England may have thought the threat from Napoleon was over. Collingwood knew that Bonaparte had lost temporary control of the sea, and that the immediate threat of invasion was over, but that he was still powerful enough to rebuild his fleets, and still dominated the continental scene. Napoleon had crushed an Austro-Russian alliance at the Battle of Austerlitz in December 1805; the Navy's guard could not be dropped for an instant. While the overall strategy remained, to dominate the major trade routes and provoke the French fleet into another set-piece battle, the detail was changed. Smaller squadrons were despatched to harry ports and harbours and close the lid on illicit trade, and Collingwood began a series of subtle diplomatic manoeuvres that eventually won him high praise from his government. Elsewhere there was good news in actions by Duckworth in the

Caribbean and Hood off Rochefort, engaging and defeating remnants of the Cadiz and Brest squadrons.

For the time being, the Mediterranean belonged wholly to Collingwood who, isolated from his higher command structure, had to improvise his own strategy to deal with a political and military situation that was in constant flux. It was during this time that his ship – after *Royal Sovereign* returned to England he hoisted his flag in *Queen*, then *Ocean* – did not even anchor for more than a year: he wrote proudly that in all that time there had been no more than six men in the sick bay. He believed in a clean, dry ship, and in feeding his crews with fresh food whenever possible.

While Collingwood watched Cadiz and Gibraltar, Napoleon was opening a diplomatic front much further to the east that threatened the Admiral's Mediterranean strategy: France was pressurising the Turks to close the Black Sea to the Russian fleet. Collingwood sent a squadron under Vice-Admiral Duckworth to the Dardanelles, where he and the 'Diplomaticks' vacillated and failed to seize the strategic or political initiative, allowing the Turks to fortify the straits against attack from both north and south.

There was a disastrous military expedition to Egypt, which ended in failure and ignominy. It seemed that the news was bad everywhere: French armies again took Naples, and with the defeat of Austria they also held the crucial ports of Venice and Trieste in the Adriatic. By 1807, having made peace with the Russians at Tilsit, France had annexed the Ionian islands off Greece, and was threatening an invasion of Sicily. The navy had a single base – Malta – in more than 2000 miles of sea between Gibraltar and Constantinople, and from here Collingwood had to rely on small squadrons to protect vital trade against not only French, but also Algerian

Napoleon, Emperor of the French.

and other pirates. Like Nelson before him, he was desperately short of frigates.

It was now that the strategic role of Sicily began to dominate his thoughts. The Kingdom of the Two Sicilies – Naples and the extreme south of Italy together with Sicily – was a rump of the Bourbon monarchies that had been overthrown by revolution. Its rulers, King Ferdinand and Queen Maria-Carolina (sister of the decapitated Marie-Antoinette) had been briefly evacuated by Nelson in 1799 from Naples to Palermo, as Napoleon's armies over-ran Italy. Again in 1806 the French occupied Naples and this time the King and Queen fled permanently to Sicily whilst constantly intriguing with the French to recover their lost possessions. Their choice was between the devil (Bonaparte) and the deep blue sea (a British government that they believed had designs to keep Sicily as a British possession). Their court was a centre for political intrigue as well as a famously indulgent social scene.

Nelson had courted the Bourbon monarchy. Collingwood avoided them like the plague. As early as the spring of 1806 he was corresponding with the King, though. In answer to Ferdinand's pleas to protect the island, Collingwood replied that the best thing he could do to protect Sicily was to prevent the French fleet from getting out of Toulon and Cadiz, which was exactly what he was doing. He assured the King of his continued vigilance and his desire to protect Their Majesties to the utmost of his powers. The correspondence shows that they communicated as equals.

Meanwhile, General Craig had been sent to Sicily with an 8000 strong army to watch the Straits of Messina, between Sicily and the mainland, an obvious focus for attack. Like the English Channel, it only needed to be held for a day or so to ensure the safe passage of an invading force. Unlike the Channel, it was only two miles wide.

Now, deciding to allow the French out of Toulon so that he could track them and bring them to battle, Collingwood focused his thoughts on Sicily, the Adriatic and the Eastern Mediterranean, where relations with the Russians and Turks were in a constant flux. By the end of 1807 he had three squadrons posted around Sicily: at Messina, at Palermo, and himself at Syracuse.

Collingwood's first visit to Syracuse, in December 1807, was cut short by word that the French fleet was at sea. He chased them, and like Nelson in 1798, he missed them. But he was back there in January 1808, and again in March. Collingwood did briefly visit Palermo in 1808 – he wrote home that he was annoyed with himself for having left in such a hurry that his shirts were still there, being laundered. It was almost another whole year, though, before Collingwood, distracted by events elsewhere, finally met the King and Queen…

The King is a good humoured man, free and affable in his manners, and had he not unhappily been born to be a king would have been a respectable country gentleman. Matters of state weary him, and I understand he does not attend much to them. His country amusements of hunting and shooting occupy him. On the other hand, the Queen is the great politician and is continually engaged in intrigues for the recovery of their lost [kingdom] of Naples…

Such was Collingwood's control of the situation that the French Admiral Ganteaume, under the most severe pressure from his master, was never able to make a single landing in Sicily. Not for the first time, Collingwood's achievements in preventing a British possession from falling into French hands had won him discreet but heartfelt praise from the British government, whose greatest asset he proved during his last years in the Mediterranean. Once again, his strategic cunning, his diplomatic skill and his deep and thorough knowledge of the sea and his fleet's capabilities had confounded Bonaparte.

It was this period, when he was literally being worn out by worry and constant vigilance, that his obituarist was referring to later, when he wrote:

The writer has seen him upon deck without his hat, and his grey hair floating to the wind, whilst torrents of rain poured down through the shrouds, and his eye, like an eagle's, on the watch.

All through this time, Collingwood had had no leave. He had not set eyes on England since 1803, and his knowledge of events at home was confined to correspondence and a very occasional newspaper or naval gazette. He was worried, too, by some of the things he heard. He had inherited a coal mine at Chirton, near North Shields, and had to try to manage it at a distance of several thousand miles. He corresponded with the Duke of Northumberland about rights of access for his wagon ways – and interestingly, as equals, they discussed the progress of the war. Now that Sarah was a reasonably wealthy woman, and a member of society, Collingwood found that she and her father were spending considerably more money than his navy pay brought in: well beyond his means, in fact; he was concerned, too, that his daughters' education was being sacrificed to an endless round of social gatherings and frivolous pursuits. There was little he could

The Kingdom of the Two Sicilies – Naples, Sicily and the extreme south of Italy – was ruled by a remnant of the Bourbon monarchy. Sicily was in a strategic position but Collingwood prevented the French from making a single landing there.

do to influence events at home, so irregular was his contact.

One person he still thought about often was his old flame, Mary Moutray. Even now, more than twenty years after they had met in Antigua, he was writing to her, and his letters were as warm as ever:

MY DEAR FRIEND – I wish you had one of those fairy telescopes that can look into the hearts and souls of people a thousand leagues off, then might you see how much you possess my mind and how sincere an interest I take in whatever relates to your happiness and that of your dear Kate.

Collingwood's health was failing: he was working himself to death. Between May of 1807 and June 1808 he wrote letters, despatches and orders from the following locations: Gibraltar, Sardinia, Sicily, Malta and Imbro; in August of 1807 he was in the Dardanelles sorting out the mess left by Duckworth; then to Tenedos and Matapan, then Syracuse; then Palermo, Mauritimo and Corfu, where he later succeeded brilliantly in kicking the French out. In January 1808 he was back at Syracuse, then in April he was at Menorca, as relations between France and Spain deteriorated and the Spanish began to look cautiously for aid to the British. Then he sailed back to Sicily, then to Cadiz, and for a while after that he was back on his old stamping ground, the Toulon blockade. It was a staggering tour of duty. One can only be amazed that it didn't kill him before it did.

An admiral, late 18th century.

Collingwood House 1809-1810

In one of those subtle shifts of fortune whose effects only become clear much later, the focus of the Mediterranean war shifted from east to west in the summer of 1808. On May 2nd Spain, who had been a friend to France, then an ally, then a slave, rose against Napoleon. It was an ill-organised uprising, without clear objectives, and for several years it was unclear whether it would succeed; but it crucially forced Bonaparte to turn his attention from events elsewhere, and slowly but surely it drew more and more of his resources away from planned attacks on Sicily, Turkey and Egypt.

Collingwood was quick to exploit the situation. By the second week of June he was at Cadiz, offering the Spanish the support of his fleet. His arrival combined pathos and farce. Forty thousand people turned out to cheer him – not just because the British were potential liberators, but because his magnanimous conduct towards Spanish sailors after Trafalgar had won him an admiring reputation. He advised the Junta on defensive measures, and offered to aid the uprising by harrying French coastal forces. Then, when they asked him if he could spare them any gunpowder, he scoured the fleet for supplies. Shortly afterwards, the same gunpowder was used to illuminate Cadiz for the feast of a local saint. Collingwood was not amused.

Even now, in his decline, Collingwood took the time to bring on young talent, though from Collingwood's pen we hear more of his failures than his successes:

But you may have heard that I am reckoned rather queer in the promotion of young men. I advance a great many who have not a friend to speak for them, while those I respect most in the world sometimes plead in vain. Those who are diligent and promise to be useful officers never miscarry. And if your friend is such an one send him to me…

… Mrs Currel's son never can be a sailor: he has something very odd in his manner, or rather he has no manner at all, but saunters a melancholic for a week together, unnoticing and unnoticed, except when I give him a little rally to make his blood circulate, and this I do, not in the expectation that it will make him better in his profession, but merely for his health's sake. It is a pity she had not put him apprentice to Jno. Wilson, the apothecary; he might have gone on very wisely. His gravity would have established his reputation as a learned doctor, and if he did poison an old woman now and then, better do that than drown an entire ship's company at a dash by running on the rocks.

[P.S.] **Bounce desires his best respects to your dogs.**

If his junior officers felt the lash of his wit, they were not alone. He thought little more of generals, of whom he had had bitter experience, from Boston to the Bosphorus. Of a fellow Northumbrian he wrote to his sister..

What do you think of your cousin Gen. Clavering? What a delightful head that man must have for the front rank of an army! It needs no helmet, they might hack their swords to saws without harm to it. I always thought Sir Thomas had the most distinguished head in that family, but I have been mistaken.

Meanwhile, both he and the British government, seizing the moment, realised that now was their chance to utilise a former asset in Menorca, and by September 1808 – as Sir Arthur Wellesley (later the Duke of Wellington) was making his first grand entrance onto the European stage at Vimeiro in Portugal, the Spanish again allowed the British fleet to anchor there and repair their ships. It was a vital advantage. The island had long been recognised as strategically valuable to any country which could possess it. Not only did it lie centrally between Spain, France, Italy and Corsica and Sardinia, but it boasted the finest deep-water harbour in the Mediterranean at Mahon. In the late 17th century the British had established a naval facility there: a careening station for cleaning ships' hulls, an ordnance yard and hospital, and other port services. For much of the 18th century Menorca remained a British possession under a variety of sometimes just, sometimes arrogant governors.

For the last two years of his life Collingwood was frequently at Port Mahon, a port he knew well from his days in *Liverpool*. It was a convenient place to gather intelligence and from which to conduct his complicated naval and diplomatic strategies. He still held the increasingly faint hope that he could catch a large French fleet at sea and defeat them

decisively, having several times already narrowly missed them because of bad weather or poor intelligence. Having a fleet at Port Mahon gave him one last chance, and in 1809 he took it. Oddly, it was on October 21st 1809, the fourth anniversary of Trafalgar, that news came of the French leaving Toulon. In an action off Rosas Bay, on a smaller scale, but nevertheless important, five French convoy ships were burned and two ships of the line were driven ashore.

At what point Collingwood took or bought the house then called El Fonduco, between Mahon and Villa Carlos (now Es Castell), is not known. He usually stayed aboard his flagship – first *Ocean*, then *Ville de Paris*, but at some point during the autumn of 1809 he came ashore and stayed for a substantial period; doctors advised him to try riding a horse and taking a little exercise. A letter written, perhaps, from El Fonduco (now Collingwood House) in January 1810 shows that it was the longest spell he had spent ashore since leaving England nearly seven years before. By now, poor Bounce was dead, having been washed overboard during a storm on the Toulon blockade. He (or a successor with the same name) had been with Collingwood for 19 years. His master would not be long in following.

Collingwood House was a perfect shore base. It lay a mile to the south-east of Mahon, away from crowds and noisy sailors. It overlooked a secure anchorage where he could see his flagship, and it was large and comfortable, with enough room for conferences with his captains and local politicians. A short walk to the cliff top, and a set of rock-hewn steps brought him down to the cove of El Fonduco from where his bargemen could row him out to his ship with a minimum of fuss.

Sick, tired, and knowing he was dying, and after repeated

requests to return to England had – very flatteringly – been turned down, Collingwood resigned his command on February 22nd 1810, and on the 25th was rowed out to his ship. She was windbound for a few days but finally, on March 6th, she was warped out of the harbour and set sail for England. Collingwood died the next evening at sea.

In the wars against Napoleon, from 1793 until 1815, Britain was able to rely on four great commanders who, among many thousands of soldiers and sailors, were pre-eminent in their vision, skills, bravery and sense of duty. They followed each other in an exact sequence: first Earl St Vincent, architect of British naval strategy; then Nelson, brilliant battle commander and unsubtle but effective diplomatist. On

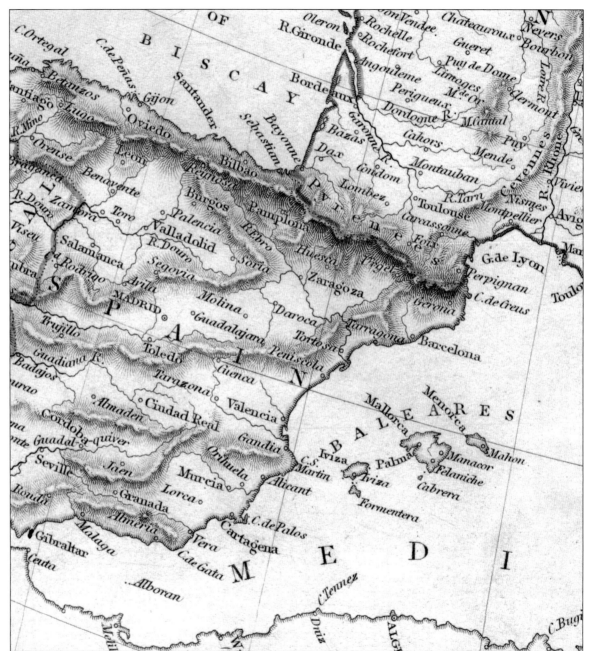

Menorca was a strategically valuable base with a fine harbour at Mahon.

Max Adams

Nelson's death Collingwood became the supreme commander of the effort against Napoleon, and on his death, the focus of the war moved squarely to the Iberian Peninsula where Wellington would triumph three years later.

In summing up the achievements of Collingwood's last years, one historian has written:

The naval history of the years after Trafalgar is not of battles. The fights were small fierce encounters of sloops and gunboats, cutting-out expeditions, attacks on batteries. Only once did the enemy come out in force. Yet the scale was heroic; and over the vast canvas towers the figure of Collingwood.

In the *Newcastle Courant* of April 21st 1810, we read:

A mail from Gibraltar and Cadiz arrived on Tuesday; it has brought intelligence which will be received with the deepest concern, viz. the death of our highly distinguished and gallant townsman, Admiral Lord Collingwood. His health had long been in a declining state, but he persisted in keeping the sea, being anxious to bring the Toulon fleet to action, and by the defeat of the last naval force of the enemy, to complete the destruction of the French navy. At length his health declined so much that he was under the necessity of determining to return to England. It pleased heaven, however, that he should see his native land no more. On the 6th ult. He left Menorca, on board the Ville de Paris, and on the 7th he breathed his last. Leaving only two daughters, the title dies with His Lordship; but his services will forever live in the memory of a grateful country.

And then a week later…

On Saturday last, the Nereus frigate arrived at the Great Nore, with the remains of the late Lord Collingwood. They are now lying in state, in the royal hospital for seamen at Greenwich, and are to be entombed in St. Paul's cathedral, with those of His Lordship's illustrious friend and commander NELSON. A monument will be erected by the public, in the same place, in grateful memory of his services.

Collingwood is not only commemorated in St Paul's, but also at Tynemouth, and there is a cenotaph in St Nicholas' Cathedral in Newcastle on which, every Trafalgar Day, a wreath is laid in his honour. A bust looks down from the site of his birthplace on the Side; his house can still be seen at Morpeth. And in a thousand Northumbrian hedgerows grow the oaks that he planted so that his country should never again want for warships.

The Collingwood Memorial by Rossi, erected 1821, in St Nicholas' Cathedral, photographed in its original position in the nave around 1930. It is now near the entrance. There is also a stone in memory of Sarah Collingwood, who died in 1819, in the nave.

Further reading

Abram, D. 2000 *The Rough Guide to Corsica*. Rough Guides

Adams, M. 2005 Admiral Collingwood: Nelson's own hero. Weidenfield & Nicholson.

Andrews, R. and Brown, J. 2002 *The Rough Guide to Sicily*. Rough Guides

Ayling, S. 1972 *George the Third*. Collins

Coleman, T. 2001 *Nelson*. Bloomsbury

Country Life 1978 *The Country Life Book of Nautical terms under sail*. London: Country Life

Fraser, C.M. and Emsley, K 1973 *Tyneside*. David and Charles

Hay, M.D. (Ed) 1958 *Landsman Hay: the memoirs of Robert Hay 1789-1847*. Rupert Hart-Davis

Howarth, D. 1969 *Trafalgar: the Nelson touch*. London: Collins

Hughes, E. 1957 *The private correspondence of Admiral Lord Collingwood*. Navy Records Society.

Ireland, B. 2000 *Naval warfare in the age of sail*. London: Harper Collins

Ketchum, R. M. 1962 *Decisive day: the battle for Bunker Hill*. Owl Books

Lee, P. 2001 *The Rough guide to Menorca*. Rough Guides

Lewis, J.E. 2000 *The mammoth book of life before the mast*. Robinson

Mackesy, P. 1957 *The War in the Mediterranean 1803-1810*.

Newnham Collingwood, G.L. 1828 *A selection from the public and private correspondence of Vice-Admiral Lord Collingwood, interspersed with memoirs of his life*. 3rd Edition. London

Oliver, T. 1831 *A picture of Newcastle upon Tyne*. Dover Publications

Parsons, G.S. 1843 *Nelsonian reminiscences: Leaves from memory's log*. Saunders and Otley

Raigersfeld, J. Baron de, 1929 *The life of a sea officer*. Cassell & co

Rodger, N.A.M. 1986 *The wooden world: an anatomy of the Georgian navy*. London: Fontana

Vaitilingam, A. 2001 *The Rough Guide to Antigua and Barbuda*. Rough Guides

Warner, O. 1968 *The life and letters of Vice-Admiral Lord Collingwood*. London: OUP

Contemporary engravings have been reproduced from books in Newcastle Libraries:

Ancient and Modern Ships by George C.V. Holmes, 1900
The British Tar by Charles Napier Robinson, 1909
The British Fleet by Charles Napier Robinson, 1894
The Naval Chronology of Great Britain by J. Ralfe, 1820
A New History of the Twenty Year War with France by Hewson Clarke 3v, 1816.
Various woodcuts by Thomas Bewick and his contemporaries from collections in Newcastle Libraries and from: *Falconer's Celebrated Marine Dictionary*, abridged 1930. In Max Adams' collection.

Index of names

Index of ships